Alfred Jarry

THE UBU PLAYS

UBU REX
(Ubu Roi)

translated by Cyril Connolly and Simon Watson Taylor

UBU CUCKOLDED
(Ubu Cocu)

translated by Cyril Connolly

UBU ENCHAINED
(Ubu Enchaîné)

translated by Simon Watson Taylor

with
Writings on the Theatre

edited, with an introduction, by Simon Watson Taylor

Methuen Drama

METHUEN WORLD CLASSICS

The Ubu Plays first published in this English edition by
Methuen & Co. Ltd 1968
Reprinted 1972, 1976, 1977, 1978, 1980, 1981, 1984 and 1987
Reprinted in 1989 by Methuen Drama
an imprint of Reed Consumer Books Ltd
Michelin House, 81 Fulham Road, London SW3 6RB
and Auckland, Melbourne, Singapore and Toronto
and distributed in the United States of America by Heinemann,
a division of Reed Publishing (USA) Inc.,
361 Hanover Street, Portsmouth, New Hampshire NH 03801 3959

Reprinted 1991
Reissued in the Methuen World Classics series in 1993

This translation: *Ubu Rex*
copyright © 1968 Cyril Connolly and Simon Watson Taylor

This translation: *Ubu Cuckolded*
copyright © 1965 by Cyril Connolly

Introduction and this translation: *Ubu Enchained*
copyright © 1968 by Simon Watson Taylor

Writings on the Theatre, first published in
Selected Works of Alfred Jarry by Methuen & Co.,
copyright © 1965 by Roger Shattuck and Simon Watson Taylor

Printed and bound in Great Britain by
Cox & Wyman Ltd, Reading, Berkshire

ISBN 413-67990-X

Contents

Alfred Henri Jarry

1873   Born September 8th (Feast of the Nativity of the Holy Virgin) in Laval (Mayenne), the second child of Anselme Jarry, merchant, and his wife Caroline, née Quernest.

1878-9   Attends the Laval *petit lycée*.

1879   Caroline Jarry leaves her husband, taking Alfred and his elder sister Charlotte with her to live with her father in Saint-Brieuc (Côtes du Nord). Alfred attends the Saint-Brieuc *lycée* 1879-88. During 1885-8 writes his first verse and prose sketches, lampoons on his teachers and fellow-pupils.

1888-91   Enters the Rennes *lycée* in October 1888. Becomes friendly with a fellow-pupil, Henri Morin, and adds his contribution to the saga LES POLONAIS, written by Henri and his elder brother Charles, satirizing their physics teacher, M. Hébert. This primitive version of UBU ROI is performed by the marionettes of the 'Théâtre des Phynances', first at the Morins' home, then from 1890 onwards at the Jarrys'. During these years he writes (with the probable collaboration of Henri Morin) ONÉSIME OU LES TRIBULATIONS DE PRIOU, which is the original version of UBU COCU and is also performed by the Théâtre des Phynances.

1891-3   Moves to Paris in October 1891 to attend the course of *rhétorique supérieure* at the Lycée Henri IV. During these years various live performances are given, at his lodgings, of early versions of UBU ROI and UBU COCU, in which Pa Ubu first acquires his name. In April 1893, first publication, in the monthly review *L'Echo de Paris*, of a text by Jarry, GUIGNOL (another early version of UBU COCU).

1894   Publication of his first book, LES MINUTES DE

SABLE MÉMORIAL (which incorporates GUIGNOL). Commencement of his lifelong friendship with the publisher Alfred Vallette and his wife the novelist Rachilde. Publication, in October, of the first issue of the art review L'YMAGIER, which he founds with Remy de Gourmont, and of which he remains the co-director for the first five issues, 1894–5.

1895   Called up in June for military service, discharged for medical reasons in November. His second book, CÉSAR-ANTÉCHRIST, is published in October.

1896   Publishes two issues of a luxurious art review, PERHINDERION. Becomes administrative assistant to Lugné-Poe, director of the Théâtre de l'Œuvre, the same month, June, that UBU ROI is published in its final version. December 10th: first of two scheduled performances of UBU ROI, directed by Lugné-Poe, with music by Claude Terrasse and masks and sets by Pierre Bonnard, Sérusier, Toulouse-Lautrec, Vuillard and Jarry himself.

1897   Publication of the essay QUESTIONS DE THÉÂTRE, and of his first novel, LES JOURS ET LES NUITS, 'roman d'un déserteur'.

1898   Performance of UBU ROI at the Théâtre des Pantins by Pierre Bonnard's marionettes. Publication of L'AMOUR EN VISITES. Completes his 'roman néo-scientifique' LES GESTES ET OPINIONS DU DOC-TEUR FAUSTROLL, PATAPHYSICIEN, which re-mains unpublished during his lifetime.

1899   Completes writing his third play in the Ubu cycle, UBU ENCHAÎNÉ. Launches his satirical chronicle, the ALMANACH ILLUSTRÉ DU PÈRE UBU, illus-trated by Bonnard. Publication of L'AMOUR ABSOLU.

1900   Publication of UBU ENCHAÎNÉ.

1901   Issues the second number of the ALMANACH ILLUS-TRÉ DU PÈRE UBU. Publication of his second novel,

MESSALINE, 'roman de l'ancien Rome'. November:
first performance of UBU SUR LA BUTTE (a two-act
version with songs, for marionettes, of UBU ROI) by
the Théâtre Guignol des Gueules de Bois.

1902   Publication of his third novel, LE SURMÂLE, 'roman
moderne'.

1906   Publication of UBU SUR LA BUTTE, and of the 'un
acte comique et morale en prose et vers' PAR LA
TAILLE, both designed for the marionette theatre.
Weakened by chronic malnutrition and by the ex-
cesses of wine, absinthe and ether, leaves Paris in a
state of physical collapse for his sister Charlotte's
home in Laval. Receives the last sacraments during
May, but recovers.

1907   Publication of the three-act 'operette bouffe' LE
MOUTARDIER DU PAPE. Dies at the Hôpital de la
Charité, Paris, on November 1st (All Saints' Day).
Buried in the Bagneux cemetery.

Works by Alfred Jarry published after his death include:

1911   GESTES ET OPINIONS DU DOCTEUR FAUSTROLL,
PATAPHYSICIEN, 'roman néo-scientifique', suivi de
SPÉCULATIONS. PANTAGRUEL (with Eugène De-
molder), 'opéra bouffe en cinques actes', with music
by Claude Terrasse.

1926   LES SILÈNES, a free adaptation of Christian-
Dietrich Grabbe's three-act comedy *Scherz, Satire,
Ironie und tiefere Bedeutung*, edited by Pascal
Pia.

1943   LA DRAGONNE (completed by Charlotte Jarry),
novel.

1944   UBU COCU.

1945   OEUVRES POÉTIQUES COMPLÈTES, edited by Henri

Parisot, with a preface by André Frédérique. (Very far from 'complete'.)

1948   OEUVRES COMPLÈTES, 8 vols., edited by René Massat. (Also very far from 'complete'.)

1949   LA REVANCHE DE LA NUIT, poems, preface by Maurice Saillet.

1953   L'OBJET AIMÉ, 'pastorale en un acte', preface by Roger Shattuck.

1958   UBU, two-act condensed version of UBU ROI and UBU ENCHAÎNÉ, with songs from UBU SUR LA BUTTE, created by Jean Vilar for the production by the Théâtre Nationale Populaire.

1962   TOUT UBU, all the plays, early fragments, alternative versions, plus all the essays, notes, letters, chronicles and poems concerning Ubu, edited by Maurice Saillet.

1964   SAINT-BRIEUC DES CHOUX, juvenile verse and prose sketches, edited and with a preface by Maurice Saillet.

1972   OEUVRES COMPLÈTES D'ALFRED JARRY, Vol. I, edited by Michel Arrivé.
1978   UBU, edited by Noël Arnaud and Henri Bordillon.

Critical studies in English include:
Claude Schumacher, *Alfred Jarry and Guillaume Apollinaire* (1984)
K. S. Beaumont, *Alfred Jarry: A Critical and Biographical Study* (1984)

Critical studies in French include:
Noël Arnaud, *Alfred Jarry, d'Ubu Roi au docteur Faustroll* (1974)
François Caradec, *A la recherche d'Alfred Jarry* (1974)
Henri Béhar, *Jarry dramaturge* (1980)

Introduction

Le Père Ubu was born in 1888, the year that Alfred Jarry entered the Rennes *lycée* at the age of fifteen, and became friendly with a fellow-pupil, Henri Morin, who had been indulging in the popular classroom sport of baiting the unfortunate physics teacher, Monsieur Hébert (known to his pupils variously as 'P.H.', 'Père Heb', 'Ebé', etc.). Henri had written, together with his elder brother Charles, a short satire, *Les Polonais*, in which 'le Père Ebé' suffered unspeakable indignities as king of an imaginary Poland. Jarry converted this sketch into a playlet for marionettes, which was performed first at the home of the Morins and later at the home of the Jarrys. While at the Rennes *lycée*, Jarry developed the same promising theme in a 'pièce alquemique', *Onésime ou les Tribulations de Priou*, featuring 'le P. H.' and 'la Mère E. B.'.

After leaving Rennes for Paris in 1891 to attend the Lycée Henri IV, he rewrote both *Les Polonais* which he had inherited from the Morin brothers, and his own *Onésime* (in which the younger Morin may have collaborated), and the resulting plays, the first drafts of *Ubu Roi* and *Ubu Cocu* respectively, were performed by Jarry and a circle of school-friends (including Léon-Paul Fargue) at his lodgings in an alleyway off the Boulevard du Port-Royal. It was only now that 'le P. H.' assumed his definitive identity as 'le Père Ubu'.

In April 1893, Jarry saw his writing in print for the first time with the publication of three prose texts (two of them fragments from this proto-*Ubu Cocu*) in a literary review: from this moment, any thought of continuing his studies at the Ecole Normale Supérieure vanished, and he plunged into the world of letters. The publication in October 1894 of his first book, the ultra-symbolist *Minutes de Sable Mémorial*, by the Editions du Mercure de France, whose publisher, Alfred Vallette, and his wife the novelist Rachilde, were to remain his lifelong friends and loyal rescuers in time of need, was followed by an abbreviated period of military service, and the publication in October 1895 of his second book, *César-Antéchrist*.

In January 1896, Jarry was introduced to Lugné-Poe, the director of the Théâtre de l'Œuvre, and proposed to him the production of either *Ubu Roi* (in a revised version) or *Les Polyèdres* (his original title for the first version of *Ubu Cocu*). In June, Lugné-Poe invited Jarry to become *secrétaire-régisseur* of his company, and this same month saw the publication by Vallette of *Ubu Roi*, which was greeted by mainly favourable critical reviews. Jarry now abandoned the idea of having *Les Polyèdres* produced at the Théâtre de l'Œuvre and decided to concentrate instead on persuading Lugné-Poe to stage *Ubu Roi*. His campaign for his play eventually conquered Lugné-Poe's doubts, and it received its first performance on December 10th, 1896. The scenes of violence and pandemonium that accompanied this notorious *première* have been frequently recounted and commented upon. The theatre critics took over the battle from the screaming, whistling, fist-shaking audience the following day, and continued the duel of insults from the pages of their newspapers, while in the cafés and salons of Paris the mutual recriminations between supporters and opponents of the play raged unabated for weeks. There were two results, one long-term and the other immediate: the French theatre was never the same again; and Jarry suddenly found himself famous overnight. His friends soon began to address him as 'Père Ubu', and he reciprocated by adopting the language, manners and gait of his creation.

In 1898, *Ubu Roi* was performed again by the marionettes of the artist Pierre Bonnard's Théâtre des Pantins. It was probably during this or the previous year that Jarry completed another version of the second play in the Ubu cycle, *Ubu Cocu ou l'Archéopteryx*, but failed to find a publisher for it. Indeed neither version of *Ubu Cocu* was either published or performed during Jarry's lifetime, and the play had to wait until 1944 to see the light of day, when an edition of the second version was printed from a manuscript which had been acquired by Paul Eluard.

During 1899, Jarry worked on the third play in the Ubu

cycle, *Ubu Enchaîné*, and completed it in September. Although published the following year, it was only in 1937 that this play received its first performance, in a production by Sylvain Itkine, together with Jarry's unpublished playlet *L'Objet Aimé* as a curtain-raiser. In 1899, and again in 1901, Jarry published an *Almanach Illustré du Père Ubu* which contained pungent comments by the Master of Phynances on the world around him, illustrated wittily by Bonnard. Jarry was also engaged in re-writing *Ubu Roi* as a two-act *guignol* version, with songs, and this fourth play in the Ubu cycle, renamed *Ubu sur la Butte*, was performed in November 1901 by the marionettes of the Théâtre Guignol des Gueules de Bois, although it was not published until 1906, one year before his death.

During the fifteen short years between the first night of *Ubu Roi* and his death at the age of 34 Jarry had seen his career as a playwright checked: once the initial impact of *Ubu Roi* had worn off, it seemed that neither producers nor publishers were anxious to invest their money and reputation in the subsequent developments of the Ubu theme, and Jarry could not persuade even his closest friends in the publishing business to print more than a few fragments of *Ubu Cocu*. It must be remembered, too, that during these years Jarry was pursuing with equal singlemindedness several parallel careers, as poet, novelist, journalist, literary and art critic, artist-engraver and fine arts editor (the glorious but brief period of *L'Ymagier* and *Perhinderion*, two luxurious art reviews which soon swallowed up the modest fortune he had inherited on the death of his father), as well as playing the strenuous and deadly serious roles of court jester to the avant-garde intelligentsia, and compulsive alcoholic, under conditions of increasingly desperate poverty. His most important non-dramatic work, standing apart from but complementing the Ubu plays, was *Les Gestes et Opinions du Docteur Faustroll, Pataphysicien*, a book which defies classification and in which Jarry elaborated his Science of Pataphysics (the 'science of imaginary solutions' which 'will examine the laws governing exceptions, and will explain the universe supplementary to this one . . .'). This extraordinary, Rabelaisian 'neo-scientific novel' completely baffled even his closest friends in the literary world, and only a few chapters from the book were published, by the *Mercure de France* review, during his lifetime. Jarry himself seemed to have fore-seen this impasse when he wrote on the last page of his manu-script of *Faustroll*, under the word 'END': 'This book will not be published integrally until the author has acquired sufficient experience to savour all its beauties in full', and indeed it was not published until 1911, four years after his death. As Roger Shattuck has written: 'At twenty-five Jarry suggested he was writing over everyone's head, including his own; he had to "experience" death in order to catch up with himself.'*

This is not the place to attempt either an examination of the aims of this very complex writer, or an assessment of his im-pact on the development of twentieth-century French drama and literature,† but two basic points require to be made: first, that Alfred Jarry was, of course, very much more than the sum of his Ubus, and that the Ubu plays achieve their full dimen-sion within the context of Jarry's writings on the theatre and, indeed, his whole *œuvre*, especially *Faustroll*;‡ secondly, that the three Ubu plays are not to be taken as a simple sequence of tragi-comic farces woven around the monstrous central figure of Ubu. There is a basic affinity between *Ubu Roi* and *Ubu Cocu*, the first an adaptation by Jarry of an existing text in a continuing schoolboy saga, the second an original contribution to that same saga, and although Jarry later revised both these texts he never departed from the norms set by the small anony-

* Introduction to *Selected Works of Alfred Jarry*, edited by Roger Shattuck and Simon Watson Taylor, Methuen, London, and Grove Press, New York, 1965.

† The reader is referred to Roger Shattuck's long and illuminating essay on Alfred Jarry in his *The Banquet Years*, Doubleday, New York, 1958 and 1961, Faber & Faber, London, 1961. Martin Esslin's *Theatre of the Absurd*, Doubleday, New York, 1961, Eyre & Spottis-woode, London, 1962 and (in a revised and enlarged edition) Penguin Books, Harmondsworth, 1968, situates Jarry historically in relation to the developing avant-garde theatre of the present century.

‡ Here again, the reader is referred to *Selected Works of Alfred Jarry*, which contains all of Jarry's writings on the theatre, as well as an annotated translation of *The Exploits and Opinions of Doctor Faustroll, Pataphysician*.

mous army of juvenile satirists of the Rennes *lycée*. *Ubu Enchaîné*, on the other hand, was the mature work of a twenty-six-year-old author, a detached and consciously contrived exposition of the pataphysical identity of opposites (freedom versus slavery, in this instance) that had already been expressed spontaneously in *Ubu Cocu* and was implicit in *Ubu Roi*. The year before writing *Ubu Enchaîné* Jarry had completed *Faustroll*, thus codifying his Science of Pataphysics. He was also in a position to draw upon his experience in the professional theatre to impose a certain dramatic discipline on the structure of his new play. The three Ubus do, nevertheless, constitute a real trinity, in which – if one may coin a pious metaphor – *Ubu Roi* may be considered the Father, *Ubu Cocu* the Son, and *Ubu Enchaîné* the Holy Ghost. . . .

Finally, a word about these translations. Jarry's use of language in the Ubu plays is as unusual as the events he recounts. The schoolboy jargon, the changes in pace and style between staccato repartee and mock-Shakespearian heroic declamation, the puns and obscure jokes all present their particular problems. And then there are the ingenious verbal inventions. The highly suggestive oaths (*merdre, cornegidouille, cornephynance*), insults (*bouffresque, salopin, bourrique*) and anatomical references (*bouzine, giborgne, oneilles*) which abound, particularly in the two earlier plays, derive directly from the accumulated repertory of slang of the Hébertique saga of Rennes, and challenge one to find suitable equivalents in English. How is one to duplicate the majestic, tongue-rolling sonority of the word *merdre*, given only our bleak, unheroic 'shit' to work on? The aerated hiss of 'pschitt' provides some labial satisfaction, but can only be considered the best of several inadequate alternatives. On the other hand, Cyril Connolly's triumphant conversion of *cornegidouille* into *hornstrumpot* gave the English language a new expletive when in 1945 he first presented his version of *Ubu Cocu* in the pages of *Horizon*.

We have inserted into our joint translation of *Ubu Roi* those of the songs from the *guignol* version, *Ubu sur la Butte*, which could be easily carried over: each such excerpt is clearly indicated in the text, so that for purposes of stage production it will be a simple matter of choice as to whether or not the songs shall be incorporated. We did not complete the Ubu cycle by translating the whole of *Ubu sur la Butte*, since this two-act *guignol* reduction of *Ubu Roi* is mainly of literary interest today, even for those interested in the marionette theatre.

An indispensable companion for the student of Ubu who reads French is Maurice Saillet's impeccably scholarly *Tout Ubu* (Le Livre de Poche, Paris, 1962), which contains not only all the Ubu plays, but also a 'Chronologie du Père Ubu', the two *Almanachs du Père Ubu*, and a number of important documents concerning the triumphs and vicissitudes of the Master of Phynances, whom Cyril Connolly was once inspired to dub, prophetically, the 'Santa Claus of the Atomic Age'.

SIMON WATSON TAYLOR

*Writings on the Theatre

*Taken from *Selected works of Alfred Jarry*,
edited by Roger Shattuck and Simon Watson Taylor.
(Pub. Methuen & Co., 1965)

A Letter to Lugné-Poe*

8 January 1896

Dear Sir,

The act which we have already discussed will be delivered to you by the agreed date, that is, about the 20th. But I am writing beforehand to ask you to give some thought to a project which I would like to submit to you and which I hope may interest you. Since *Ubu Roi*, which you liked, is a complete story in itself, I could, if you liked, simplify it somewhat, and then we would have something which could not fail to be funny: you yourself found it funny when you read it without bias one way or the other.

It would be interesting, I think, to produce this (at no cost, incidentally) in the following manner:

1) Mask for the principal character, Ubu; I could get this for you, if necessary. And, in any case, I believe that you yourself have been studying the whole question of masks in the theatre.

2) A cardboard horse's head which he would hang round his neck, as they did on the medieval English stage, for the only two equestrian scenes; all these details fit in with the mood of the play, since my intention was, in any case, to write a puppet play.

3) One single stage-set or, better still, a plain backdrop, thus avoiding the raising and dropping of the curtain during the single act. A formally dressed individual would walk on stage, just as he does in puppet shows, and hang up a placard indicating where the next scene takes place. (By the way, I am absolutely convinced that a descriptive placard has far more 'suggestive' power than any stage scenery. No scenery, no array of walkers-on could really evoke 'the Polish Army marching across the Ukraine'.)

4) The abolition of crowds which usually put on a terrible collective performance and are an insult to the intelligence. So,

---

* This is one of a series of letters written by the author of *Ubu Roi* to the Director of the Théâtre de l'Œuvre concerning the theatrical project upon which they were collaborating while Jarry worked for him as a secretary, scene-shifter and small-part actor. [Translator's note.]

just a single soldier in the army parade scene, and just one in the scuffle when Ubu says 'What a slaughter, what a mob, etc. . . .'

5) Choice of a special 'accent,' or, better still, a special 'voice' for the principal character.

6) Costumes as divorced as far as possible from local colour or chronology (which will thus help to give the impression of something eternal): modern costumes, preferably, since the satire is modern, and shoddy ones, too, to make the play even more wretched and horrible.

There are only three important characters who do much talking, Ubu, Ma Ubu and Bordure. You have an actor whose appearance is exactly right for Bordure and would make a splendid contrast with Ubu's bulk – I mean the tall fellow who declaimed: 'It is my right.'

Finally, I have not forgotten that this is no more than a suggestion for you to ponder at your leisure, and I have only discussed *Ubu Roi* with you because it has the advantage of being the sort of play that most of the public will appreciate. Anyway, the other thing I am working on will soon be ready, and you will see how much better it is. But if the project I have just outlined does not seem completely absurd to you, then I would appreciate your letting me know, so that I will not be working unnecessarily on the second scheme. As we planned, neither of them will take more than three-quarters of an hour's playing time.

With best wishes for all your good work, which gave me the chance of enjoying yet another highly interesting evening yesterday.

> Alfred Jarry,
> 162, boulevard St.-Germain

Translated by Simon Watson Taylor

Of the Futility of the 'Theatrical' in the Theatre

I think the question of whether the theatre should adapt itself to the public, or the public to the theatre, has been settled once and for all. The public only understood, or looked as if they understood, the tragedies and comedies of ancient Greece because they were based on universally known fables which, anyway, were explained over and over again in every play and, as often as not, hinted at by a character in the prologue. Just as nowadays they go to hear the plays of Molière and Racine at the Comédie Française because they are always being played, even though they certainly don't really understand them. The theatre has not yet won the freedom to eject forcibly any member of the audience who doesn't understand, or to comb out the potential hecklers and hooligans from the auditorium during each interval. But we can content ourselves with the established truth that if people do fight in the theatre it will be a work of popularization they are fighting over, one that is not in the least original and is therefore more readily accessible than the original. An original work will, at least on the first night, be greeted by a public that remains bemused and, consequently, dumb.

But first nights are attended by those capable of understanding!

If we want to lower ourselves to the level of the public there are two things we can do for them – and which *are* done for them. The first is to give them characters who think as they do (a Siamese or Chinese ambassador seeing *The Miser* would bet anything that the miser would be outwitted and his money box stolen), and whom they understand perfectly. When this is the case they receive two impressions; firstly they think that they must themselves be very witty, as they laugh at what they take to be witty writing – and this never fails to happen to Monsieur Donnay's audiences. Secondly they get the impression that they are participating in the creation of the play, which relieves them of the effort of anticipating what is going to happen. The other thing we can do for them is give them a commonplace sort of plot – write about things that happen all the time to the common man, because the fact is that Shakespeare, Michelangelo, or Leonardo da Vinci are somewhat bulky; their diameter is a bit difficult to traverse because genius, intelligence, and even talent are larger than life and so inaccessible to most people.

If, in the whole universe, there are five hundred people who, compared with infinite mediocrity, have a touch of Shakespeare and Leonardo in them, is it not only fair to grant these five hundred healthy minds the same thing that is lavished on Monsieur Donnay's audiences – the relief of not seeing on the stage what they don't understand; the *active* pleasure of participating in the creation of the play and of anticipation?

What follows is a list of a few things which are particularly horrifying and incomprehensible to the five hundred, and which clutter up the stage to no purpose; first and foremost, the *decor* and the *actors*.

Decor is a hybrid, neither natural nor artificial. If it were exactly like nature it would be a superfluous duplication. . . . (We shall consider the use of nature as decor later.) It is not artificial, in the sense that it is not, for the five hundred, the embodiment of the outside world as the playwright has seen and re-created it.

And in any case it would be dangerous for the poet to impose on a public of artists the decor that he himself would conceive. In any written work there is a hidden meaning, and anyone who knows how to read sees that aspect of it that makes sense for him. He recognizes the eternal and invisible river and calls it *Anna Perenna*.* But there is hardly anyone for whom a painted backdrop has two meanings, as it is far more arduous to extract the quality from a quality than the quality from a quantity. Every spectator has a right to see a play in a decor which does not clash with his own view of it. For the general public, on the other hand, any 'artistic' decor will do, as the masses do not understand anything by themselves, but wait to be told how to see things.

* Dido's sister, who came to Rome and drowned in a river, of which she became the nymph. *Amne perenne latens, Anna Perenna vocor*. (Ovid, *Fasti*, Book III, l. 654.) [Translator's note.]

There are two sorts of decor: indoor and outdoor. Both are supposed to represent either rooms or the countryside. We shall not revert to the question, which has been settled once and for all, of the stupidity of *trompe l'œil*. Let us state that the said *trompe l'œil* is aimed at people who only see things roughly, that is to say, who do not see at all: it scandalizes those who see nature in an intelligent and selective way, as it presents them with a caricature of it by someone who lacks all understanding. Zeuxis is supposed to have deceived some birds with his stone grapes, and Titian's virtuosity hoodwinked an innkeeper.

Decor by someone who cannot paint is nearer to abstract decor, as it gives only essentials. In the same way, simplified decor picks out only relevant aspects.

We tried *heraldic* decors, where a single shade is used to represent a whole scene or act, with the characters poised harmonically *passant* against the heraldic field. This is a bit peurile, as the said colour can only establish itself against a colourless background (but it is also more accurate, since we have to take into account the prevailing red-green colour blindness, as well as other idiosyncrasies of perception). A colourless background can be achieved simply, and in a way which is symbolically accurate, by an unpainted backdrop or the reverse side of a set. Each spectator can then conjure up for himself the background he requires, or, better still, if the author knew what he was about, the spectator can imagine, by a process of exosmosis, that what he sees on the stage is the real decor. The placard brought in to mark each change in scene saves the onlooker from being regularly reminded of base 'reality' through a constant substitution of conventional sets which he really only sees properly at the moment the scene is being shifted.

In the conditions we are advocating, each piece of scenery needed for a special purpose – a window to be opened, for instance, or a door to be broken down – becomes a prop and can be brought in like a table or a torch.

The actor adapts his face to that of the character. He should adapt his whole body in the same way. The play of his features, his expressions, etc., are caused by various contractions and extensions of the muscles of his face. No one has realized that the muscles remain the same under the make-believe, made-up face, and that Mounet and Hamlet do not have the same zygomatics, even though in anatomical terms we think that they are the same man. Or else people say that the difference is negligible. The actor should use a mask to envelop his head, thus replacing it by the effigy of the CHARACTER. His mask should not follow the masks in the Greek theatre to indicate simply tears or laughter, but should indicate the nature of the character: the Miser, the Waverer, the Covetous Man accumulating crimes. . . .

And if the eternal nature of the character is embodied in the mask, we can learn from the kaleidoscope, and particularly the gyroscope, a simple means of *illuminating*, one by one or several at a time, the critical moments.

With the old-style actor, masked only in a thinly applied make-up, each facial expression is raised to a power by colour and particularly by relief, and then to cubes and higher powers by LIGHTING.

What we are about to describe was impossible in the Greek theatre because the light was vertical, or at least never sufficiently horizontal, and therefore produced a shadow under every protuberance in the mask; it was a blurred shadow, though, because the light was diffused.

Contrary to the deductions of rudimentary and imperfect logic, there is no clear shadow in those sunny countries; and in Egypt, below the tropic of Cancer, there is hardly a trace of shadow left on the face. The light was reflected vertically as if by the face of the moon, and diffused by both the sand on the ground and the sand suspended in the air.

The *footlights* illumine the actor along the hypotenuse of a right-angled triangle, the actor's body forming one of the sides of the right angle. And as the footlights are a series of luminous points, that is to say a line which, in relation to the narrowness of the front view of the actor, extends indefinitely to right and left of its intersection with the actor's plane, these footlights should be considered as a single point of light situated at an indefinite distance, as if it were *behind* the audience.

It is true that the footlights are less than an infinite distance away, so that one cannot really regard all the rays reflected by the actor (or facial expressions) as travelling along parallel lines. But in practice each spectator sees the character's mask *equally*, with the differences which are certainly negligible compared to the idiosyncrasies and different perceptive attitudes of the individual spectator. These differences cannot be attenuated, though they cancel each other out in the audience *qua* herd, which is what an audience is.

By slow nodding and lateral movements of his head the actor can displace the shadows over the whole surface of his mask. And experience has shown that the six main positions (and the same number in profile, though these are less clear) suffice for every expression. We shall not cite any examples, as they vary according to the nature of the mask, and because everyone who knows how to watch a puppet show will have been able to observe this for himself.

They are simple expressions, and therefore universal. Present-day mime makes the great mistake of using conventional mime language, which is tiring and incomprehensible. An example of this convention is the hand describing a vertical ellipse around the face, and a kiss being implanted on this hand to suggest a beautiful woman – and love. An example of universal gesture is the marionette displaying its bewilderment by starting back violently and hitting its head against a flat.

Behind all these accidentals there remains the essential expression, and the finest thing in many scenes is the impassivity of the mask, which remains the same whether the words it emits are grave or gay. This can only be compared with the solid structure of the skeleton, deep down under its surrounding animal flesh; its tragicomic qualities have always been acknowledged.

It goes without saying that the actor must have a special *voice*, the voice that is appropriate to the part, as if the cavity forming the mouth of the mask were incapable of uttering anything other than what the mask would say, if the muscles of its lips could move. And it is better for them not to move, and that the whole play should be spoken in a monotone.

And we have also said that the actor must take on the body appropriate to the part.

Transvestism has been forbidden by the Church and by art.

Witness Beaumarchais, who in one of his prefaces wrote: 'The young man does not exist who is sufficiently developed to . . .' And since women are beardless and their voices shrill all their lives, a boy of fourteen is traditionally played on the Paris stage by a twenty-year-old woman who, being six years older, has much more experience. This is small compensation for her ridiculous profile and unaesthetic walk, or for the way the outline of all her muscles is vitiated by adipose tissue, which is odious because it has a function – it produces *milk*.

Given the difference in their brains, a boy of fifteen, if you pick an intelligent one, will play his part adequately (most women are vulgar and nearly all boys are stupid, with some outstanding exceptions). The young actor Baron, in Molière's company, is an example, and there is also the whole period in the English theatre (and the whole history of the Greek theatre) when no one would have dreamed of trusting a part to a woman.

A few words on natural decors, which exist without duplication if one tries to stage a play in the open air, on the slope of a hill, near a river, which is excellent for carrying the voice, especially when there is no awning, even though the sound may be weakened. Hills are all that is necessary, with a few trees for shade. At the moment *Le Diable Marchand de Goutte* is being played out of doors, as it was a year ago, and the production was discussed some time ago in the *Mercure* by Alfred Vallette. Three or four years ago Monsieur Lugné-Poe and some friends staged *La Gardienne* at Presles, on the edge of the Isle-Adam forest. In these days of universal cycling it would not be absurd to make use of summer Sundays in the countryside to stage a few very short performances (say from two to five o'clock in the afternoon) of literature which is not too abstract – *King Lear* would be a good example; we do not understand the idea of a people's theatre. The performances should be in places not too far distant, and arrangements should be made for people who come by train, without previous planning. The places in the sun should be free (Monsieur Barrucand was writing quite recently about the free theatre), and as for the props, the bare necessities could be transported in one or several automobiles.

Translated by Barbara Wright

Preliminary Address at the
First Performance of Ubu Roi,
December 10, 1896

Ladies and Gentlemen,

It should be quite unnecessary (apart from being slightly absurd for an author to talk about his own play) for me to come up here with a few words before the production of *Ubu Roi* after so many more distinguished people have spoken kindly of it: among whom I would especially like to thank Messieurs Silvestre, Mendès, Scholl, Lorrain and Bauer – in fact, my only excuse for speaking to you now is that I am afraid that their generosity found Ubu's belly far more swollen with satirical symbols than we have really been able to stuff it with for this evening's entertainment.

The Swedenborgian Doctor Mises has quite rightly compared rudimentary works with the most perfect achievements, and embryonic forms with the most evolved creatures, pointing out that the former categories lack any element of accident, protuberance or special characteristics, leaving them a practically spherical form like the ovule or Mister Ubu; and, equally, that the latter possess so many personal attributes that they too take on a spherical form, by virtue of the axiom that the smoothest body is the one presenting the greatest number of different facets. Which is why you are free to see in Mister Ubu as many allusions as you like, or, if you prefer, just a plain puppet, a schoolboy's caricature of one of his teachers who represented for him everything in the world that is grotesque.

This is the point of view that the Théâtre de l'Œuvre is going to give you this evening. A few actors have agreed to lose their own personalities during two consecutive evenings by performing with masks over their faces so that they can mirror the mind and soul of the man-sized marionettes that you are about to see. As the play has been put on in some haste and in a spirit of friendly improvisation, Ubu has not had time to obtain his own real mask, which would have been very awkward to wear in any case, and his confederates, too, will be decked out in only approximate disguise. It was very important that, if the actors were to be as much like marionettes as possible, we should have fairground music scored for brass and gongs and megaphones – which we simply did not have time to get together. But let us not be too hard on the Théâtre de l'Œuvre: our main intention is to bring Ubu to life through the versatile genius of Monsieur Gémier, and tonight and tomorrow are the only evenings when Monsieur Ginisty – and the current production of Villiers de l'Isle-Adam – is free to let us borrow him. We are going to make do with three complete acts, followed by two acts incorporating some cuts. I have made all the cuts the actors wanted (even sacrificing several passages essential to the understanding of the play), and for their benefit I have kept in scenes which I would have been only too happy to eliminate. For, however much we may have wanted to be marionettes, we have not quite hung each character from a string, which may not necessarily have been an absurd idea but would certainly have been rather awkward for us, and in any case we were not quite sure exactly how many people were going to be available for our crowd scenes, whereas with real marionettes a handful of pulleys and strings serves to control a whole army. So in order to fill our stage you will see leading characters such as Ubu and the Czar talking to each other while prancing around on their cardboard horses (which, incidentally, we have been up all night painting). At least the first three acts and the closing scenes will be played in full, just as they were written.

And we also have the ideal setting, for just as a play can be set in Eternity by, say, letting people fire revolvers in the year one thousand or thereabouts, so you will see doors opening onto snow-covered plains under blue skies, mantelpieces with clocks on them swinging open to turn into doorways, and palm trees flourishing at the foot of beds so that little elephants perching on bookshelves can graze on them.

As for our non-existent orchestra, we shall have to conjure up in our imagination all its sound and fury, contenting ourselves meanwhile with a few drums and pianos executing Ubu's themes from the wings.

And the action, which is about to start, takes place in Poland, that is to say Nowhere.

Translated by Simon Watson Taylor

Theatre Questions

What conditions are indispensable to the theatre? I do not think we need give any more thought to the question of whether the three unities are necessary or whether the unity of action alone will suffice, and if everything revolves around a single character then the unity of action has had its due. Nor do I think that we can argue either from Aristophanes or Shakespeare if it is the public's susceptibilities that we are supposed to respect, since many editions of Aristophanes have footnotes on every page stating: 'The whole of this passage is full of obscene allusions,' and, as for Shakespeare, one only has to reread certain of Ophelia's remarks, or the famous scene (nearly always cut) in which a Queen is taking French lessons.

The alternative would appear to be to model ourselves on Messieurs Augier, Dumas *fils*, Labiche, etc., whom we have had the misfortune to read, and with profound tedium: it is more than likely that the members of the younger generation, though they may have read these gentlemen, have not the slightest recollection of having done so. I do not think there is the slightest reason to give a work dramatic form unless one has invented a character whom one finds it more convenient to let loose on a stage than to analyse in a book.

And anyway, why should the public, which is illiterate by definition, attempt quotations and comparisons? It criticized *Ubu Roi* for being a vulgar imitation of Shakespeare and Rabelais, because 'its sets are economically replaced by a placard' and a certain word is repeated. People ought not to be unaware of the fact that it is now more or less certain that never, at least never in Shakespeare's day, have his plays been acted in any other way than with sets and on a relatively perfected stage. Furthermore, people saw *Ubu* as a work written in 'old French' because we amused ourselves by printing it in old-style type, and they thought 'phynance' was sixteenth-century spelling. I find so much more accurate the remark of one of the Poles in the crowd scenes, who said that in his opinion: 'It's just like Musset, because the set changes so frequently.'

It would have been easy to alter *Ubu* to suit the taste of the Paris public by making the following minor changes: the opening word would have been Blast (or Blasttr), the unspeakable brush would have turned into a pretty girl going to bed, the army uniforms would have been First Empire style, Ubu would have knighted the Czar, and various spouses would have been cuckolded – but in that case it would have been filthier.

I intended that when the curtain went up the scene should confront the public like the exaggerating mirror in the stories of Madame Leprince de Beaumont, in which the depraved saw themselves with dragons' bodies, or bulls' horns, or whatever corresponded to their particular vice. It is not surprising that the public should have been aghast at the sight of its ignoble other self, which it had never before been shown completely. This other self, as Monsieur Catulle Mendès has excellently said, is composed 'of eternal human imbecility, eternal lust, eternal gluttony, the vileness of instinct magnified in tyranny; of the sense of decency, the virtues, the patriotism and the ideals peculiar to those who have just eaten their fill.' Really, these are hardly the constituents for an amusing play, and the masks demonstrate that the comedy must at the most be the macabre comedy of an English clown, or of a Dance of Death. Before Gémier agreed to play the part, Lugné-Poe had learned Ubu's lines and wanted to rehearse the play as a *tragedy*. And what no one seems to have understood – it was made clear enough, though, and constantly recalled by Ma Ubu's continually repeated: 'What an idiotic man! . . . What a sorry imbecile!' – is that Ubu's speeches were not meant to be full of witticisms, as various little ubuists claimed, but of stupid remarks, uttered with all the authority of the Ape. And in any case the public, who protest with bogus scorn that it contains 'not a scrap of wit from beginning to end,' are still less capable of understanding anything profound. We know, from our four years' observation of the public at the Théâtre de l'Œuvre, that if you are absolutely determined to give the public an inkling of something you must explain it to them beforehand.

The public do not understand *Peer Gynt*, which is one of the most lucid plays imaginable, any more than they understand Baudelaire's prose or Mallarmé's precise syntax. They know nothing of Rimbaud, they only heard of Verlaine's existence after he was dead, and they are terrified when they hear *Les Flaireurs* or *Pelléas et Mélisande*. They pretend to think writers and artists a lot of crackpots, and some of them would like to purge all works of art of everything spontaneous and quintessential, of every sign of *superiority*, and to bowdlerize them so that they could have been written by the *public in collaboration*. That is their point of view, and that of certain plagiarists, conscious and unconscious. Have we no right to consider the public from our point of view? – the public who claim that we are madmen suffering from a surfeit of what they regard as hallucinatory sensations produced in us by our exacerbated senses. From our point of view it is they who are the madmen, but of the opposite sort – what scientists would call idiots. They are suffering from a dearth of sensations, for their senses have remained so rudimentary that they can perceive nothing but immediate impressions. Does progress for them consist in drawing nearer to the brute beast or in gradually developing their embryonic cerebral convolutions?

Since Art and the public's Understanding are so incompatible, we may well have been mistaken in making a direct attack on the public in *Ubu Roi*; they resented it because they understood it only too well, whatever they may say. Ibsen's onslaught on crooked society was almost unnoticed. It is because the public are a mass – inert, obtuse, and passive – that they need to be shaken up from time to time so that we can tell from their bear-like grunts where they are – and also where they stand. They are pretty harmless, in spite of their numbers, because they are fighting against intelligence. Ubu did not debrain all the nobles. They are like Cyrano de Bergerac's Icicle-Animal, which does battle with the Fire-Beast – in any case they would melt before they won, but even if they did win they would be only too honoured to hang the corpse of the sun-beast up against their mantelpieces and to allow its rays to illuminate their adipose tissue. It is a being so different from them that its relation to them is like an exterior soul to their bodies.

Light is active and shade is passive, and light is not detached from shade but, given sufficient time, penetrates it. Reviews which used to publish Loti's novels are now printing a dozen pages of Verhaeren and several of Ibsen's plays.

Time is necessary because people who are older than we – and whom we respect for that reason – have lived among certain works which have the charm of habitual objects for them, and they were born with the souls that match these works, guaranteed to last until eighteen-ninety . . . odd. We shall not try to push them out of our way – we are no longer in the seventeenth century; we shall wait until their souls, which made sense in relation to themselves and to the false values which surrounded them throughout their lives, have come to a full stop (even though we have not waited). We too shall become solemn, fat, and Ubu-like and shall publish extremely classical books which will probably lead to our becoming mayors of small towns where, when we become academicians, the blockheads constituting the local intelligentsia will present us with Sèvres vases, while they present their moustaches on velvet cushions to our children. And another lot of young people will appear, and consider us completely out of date, and they will write ballads to express their loathing of us, and that is just the way things should always be.

Translated by Barbara Wright

Twelve Theatrical Topics

1) The dramatist, like all other artists, is searching for the truth – which exists in several different versions. And as the first glimmerings were acknowledged as incorrect, it is quite likely that over the last few years the theatre has been able to discover – or to create, which comes to the same thing – several new dimensions of eternity. And when it has not been able to discover anything new, then it has rediscovered and reunderstood the classic Greek theatre.

2) Dramatic art has been born all over again – or maybe just simply born in France – during the last few years, so far having only let us see *Les Fourberies de Scapin* (and Bergerac, of course) and *Les Burgraves*. Among us is a tragic man, possessing new terrors and pities, all so private and personal that it would be pointless for him to express them in any other way but silence: his name is Maurice Maeterlinck. And then there is Charles Van Lerberghe. And other names we will quote later. We feel absolutely certain that we are witnessing a theatrical birth, for in France for the first time (or in *Belgium*, rather, at Ghent, because for us France is not some inanimate territory, but a language, and Maeterlinck belongs to us just as legitimately as Mistral does not) there is an ABSTRACT theatre, and at last we can enjoy something which may be as eternally tragic as Ben Jonson, Marlowe, Shakespeare, Cyril Tourneur or Goethe without the bother of a translation. All that is missing is a play as crazy as the only one that Dietrich Grabbe ever wrote, and which has never been translated.

The Théâtre d'Art, the Théâtre Libre and the Œuvre have presented, along with a few inevitable duds (*Théodat*, etc.), translations of foreign plays that were new because they expressed new feelings: Ibsen, translated by Count Prozor, and those strange adaptations from Sanskrit by A-F Hérold and Barrucand. These companies have also discovered dramatists like Rachilde, Pierre Quillard, Jean Lorrain, F Sée, Henry Bataille, Maurice Beauborg,

Paul Adam and Francis Jammes, several of whom have written works practically justifying the title of masterpieces, and which in any case have broken new ground and proclaimed their authors as genuine creators.

With a few others, and several old masters about to be translated (Marlowe by G. E.*), they will all be put on this season at the Œuvre, while Aeschylus is being retranslated at the Odéon, on the principle that as thought goes round in circles there is nothing quite so up-to-date as a very, very old play.

And a few fine starts have been made on scenery by artists at various private theatres, as can be discovered in an article by Monsieur Lugné-Poe which appeared on the first of October in the *Mercure*, and in which he discussed a not impracticable scheme for an 'Elizabethan Theatre.'

3) What is a play? A public holiday? A lesson? A pastime? In the first place it might seem that a play ought to be a kind of public holiday, being a show put on for a crowd of citizens gathered together. But we must not forget that there are several different kinds of theatre audiences, or at least two: there is the audience of a few intelligent people, and the one that is just a crowd. For the crowd, spectacular shows (with scenery and dancing and visible and tangible emotions – at the Châtelet and the Gaité, the Ambigu and the Opéra-Comique) are mainly a pastime, and maybe just a little bit of a lesson since they are not forgotten quite immediately, but a lesson in mock sentimentality and mock aesthetics, which are the only real kind for people like that, and for whom the minority theatre seems an incomprehensible bore. This other theatre is neither a holiday for its audience, nor a lesson, nor a pastime – it is something real: the elite join in the creation of one of themselves who, among this elite, sees a being come to life in himself that was created by himself: an active pleasure which is God's sole pleasure and which the holiday mob achieves in caricature in the carnal act.

But even they enjoy this creative pleasure in their own small way. I refer you to my article in the *Mercure de France* of September, '96 on the 'Futility of the "Theatrical" in the

* Georges Eekhoud, who translated *Edward II* into French for Lugné-Poe. [Editor's note.]

Theatre': 'If we want to lower ourselves . . . and of anticipation?'*

4) Obviously anything can be put on the stage if we are still going to give the name of theatres to those places cluttered with messily painted scenery, specially constructed, like the plays, for the masses. But, having made this clear, let us also say that the only person who ought to be allowed to write for the theatre is the man who thinks primarily in dramatic terms. People can make novels out of plays later on, if they want to, because dramatic action can be narrated; but the other way round almost never succeeds; and if a novel happens to be dramatic, then the author should have thought of it and written it as a play in the first place.

The theatre, bringing impersonal masks to life, is only for those who are virile enough to create new life; either as a conflict of passions subtler than those we already know, or as a complete new character. It is obvious that Hamlet, say, is more alive than the man in the street, being both more complicated and more integrated, and perhaps he is the only one really alive, for he is a walking abstraction. Therefore it is harder for the mind to create a character than for matter to create a man; and if we are absolutely incapable of creating and giving birth to a new being, then we would do better to keep quiet.

5) Stage fashions and street fashions obviously have much influence on each other – and not only in modern plays. But there would not be much point in an audience turning up at the theatre in party dress: actually it does not matter that much, but it is aggravating to find people peering round to see what everyone else in the theatre is wearing. Don't people go to Bayreuth dressed for the journey? The whole question could easily be solved by never putting up the lights in the auditorium!

6) A recent best-seller [Courteline's *Les Linottes*] has come out strongly in favour of the '*ten o'clock theatre*'. But there will always be people to drown the opening scenes of a play with the noises they make coming in late. The present time for raising the curtain is all right, so long as we make sure that all the doors are shut – not only to the auditorium, but to the corridors leading to it too – as soon as the lights have dimmed.

---

* See p. xxi, para 3 *seq.* [Editor's note.]

7) Writing a part with the talents of a particular actor in mind is the method most likely to result in ephemeral plays: for, once that actor is dead, it will not be easy to find an identical replacement. This system gives an author without creative talent the advantage of a ready-made model whose muscles he can flex as he chooses. Really, the actor (with a minimum of education) might just as well talk about himself and say whatever he liked. The weakness of this system is most obvious in the tragedies of Racine, which are not really plays, but rosaries of roles. It is not 'stars' that are needed, but a homogeneous array of sombre masks: docile silhouettes.

8) The virtue of dress rehearsals is that they are a free show for a select group of artists and friends of the author, and where for one unique evening the audience is almost completely expurgated of idiots.

9) The part played by 'little theatres' is not yet over, but as they have been running for several years now, people have stopped finding them crazy, and a certain few have made them their regular theatre. In a few years' time we will have come nearer the truth in art, or (if it is not a truth but just another fashion) we will have discovered another version of it, and these theatres will have become regular in the worst sense of the word unless they remember that their whole point is not in being but in becoming.

10) To keep up even a worthwhile tradition means vitiating the idea behind it which must necessarily be in a constant state of evolution: it is mad to try to express new feelings in a 'mummified' form.

11) Let us keep academic training for revivals, if you like, but even then, can we be sure that the audience, whose ideas are also in process of evolution, even if there is always a time lag of a few years, will not insist that the means of expression be brought up to date too? Classical plays were acted in the costume of the day; let us do the same as those old painters who tried to give even the most ancient historical scenes a contemporary appearance.

All 'historical' stuff is a boring nuisance, i.e., useless.

12) Reproduction rights are vested in the author's descendants, thus involving the institution of the family – a matter in which we readily admit our own incompetence. Is it better for descendants to possess reproduction rights and then suppress works as they

wish, or for masterpieces, once their authors are dead, to become public property? The present arrangement seems best to me. – In second-rate touring shows, for instance, the paid *claque* allows the author to indicate to his audience how he intended them to appreciate his play. It is a safety valve to prevent unruly enthusiasm breaking out when it should not. But paid applause is a kind of stage direction for the audience; in a theatre which is really a theatre and where a play is being done which . . . etc., we believe, along with Monsieur Maeterlinck, that the applause of silence is the only kind that counts.

Translated by Stanley Chapman

Concerning Inverse Mimicry in the Characters of Henri De Régnier

We know that certain animals use a phenomenon called 'mimicry' to hide themselves from their enemies: one butterfly, in order not to be recognized as a butterfly, *imitates* a dead leaf; and there is no doubt about the fact that it does so deliberately, and, if not as the result of a decision based on the experience of its own ephemeral existence, then surely through the genuine scientific knowledge acquired during the myriads of centuries of which it is the end product, this knowledge being much older and farther advanced than that exercised by man. Therefore, if, in order to become indistinguishable from the environment in which it wants to go on living – for 'living' is meaningless without continuity – the animal apes its surroundings, it is because it admits to being weaker than they are: it respects the power of what is – or what it considers to be – invulnerable, since it knows they will live longer than itself. But, in contrast, the characters created by Henri de Régnier, which will endure, especially since we are now proving their durability, do better still: in some strange way their exuberant personalities exude their own special surroundings which could not possibly have any existence at all without them. Their muscles are of stone, yet they never become petrified, since for century after century they have continued to live in stone dwellings in the same place like gigantic trees. They congeal their surroundings into their own image and erect palaces of space around themselves. They never take a step without the effulgence of a halo following and magnifying their outline. But since these characters think and speak, each with his own set of rules, and since we see them from the inside, the iridescent wrapping of their personal scenery does not shield them from us. Each facet of that corner of the universe in which they like to be remembers them like a melody, because they *are*, and this gives a musical radiance to their surrounding aura. Since the human spirit is not yet sufficiently developed to comprehend or follow divergent rays to infinity, these rays culminate in a symbol of the limitation of our powers: a corona. In another kind of vibration, they would be portraits, spinning the gilt of their frames to their own measurements as they sit.

Thus, Monsieur de Hangsdorff, the collector of antique glass, rather than conform with his surroundings, has chosen to surround himself with things that are in harmony with him. He is 'short and tubby, like a gourd. His head, bald as a champagne cork, seemed to be a stopper to his body's jug, which was completed by the handles formed by his arms. His hands were soft and damp as if specially made like that in order to grip the glass and hold it better.'

Like ripples spreading from a pebble thrown into water, the things influenced by the individual become more and more numerous. Venice, the town of motionless water – and what is glass if not a motionless water, and can one not, by straining it through a glass funnel, remove the water from the wine, in the same way as one might pick out bits of broken crystal? – Venice captivates Hangsdorff.

The bells there are chinking goblets. We are quite surprised to find Monsieur de Hangsdorff 'growing suddenly gloomy when he thinks of the double cannon-shot fired at noon and at eight o'clock every evening from San Giorgio Maggiore'. The vibration should surely be an ideal twice-daily check to delight the owner of a faultless collection. Since it is the bare outline of themselves and their absolute which is 'in charge,' Hangsdorff and Serpigny admirably – that is, fatally – 'sip a sherbet which was like ground glass'.

And if every hero brings his own scenery with him, and if we never see the Prince of Praizig without his military greatcoat, Madame de Vitry without her rouge, the lovable old Prince of Bercenay without his walking stick, fat Bocquincourt without some portion of his flesh showing through his clothes, Monsieur Baragon without untied shoelaces for him to trip over, nor Madame Brignan without her dyed hair, then this proves, and no more evidence is needed, that the author has turned his creatures inside out and exposed their soul: the soul is a nervous tic.

Homer, or whoever signed his works, was a great psychologist in never forgetting to add to each name its epithet: from this sprang the first and best 'canting arms'. And if characters are presented to us through their masks, let us not forget that 'character' means simply 'mask,' and that the 'false face' is the true one, since it is the only personal one. A writer must be very cautious and very sure of himself if, for his ends, he uses only one feature of the mask; but we shall not complain since we are dealing with somebody who knows how to choose. With Cleopatra the nose is enough: we know that the rest will follow – and not very far behind.

Translated by Stanley Chapman

Ubu Rex

(Ubu Roi)

Drama in five Acts
in prose
Restored in its entirety
as it was performed by
the marionettes of the Théâtre
des Phynances in 1888

Translated by Cyril Connolly and Simon Watson Taylor

COMPOSITION OF THE ORCHESTRA*

Oboes

Pipes

Saveloys

Enormous Double-bass

Flageolets   Transverse Flutes

Concert Flute

Little Bassoon   Big Bassoon

Triple Bassoon   Little black Cornets

High-pitched white Cornets

Horns   Sackbuts   Trombones

Green ivory Hunting-horns   Fipple-flutes

Bagpipes

Bombardons   Kettledrums

Drum   Bass Drum

Grand Organs

* Taken from the autographic facsimile edition of *Ubu Roi*, text by Alfred Jarry and music by Claude Terrasse (Mercure de France, 1897).

This Book
is dedicated
to
MARCEL SCHWOB

Thereatte Lord Ubu shooke his peare-head, whence he
is by the Englysshe yclept Shakespeare, and you have from
him under thatte name many goodlie tragedies
in his own hande.

CHARACTERS

PA UBU
MA UBU
CAPTAIN MACNURE
KING WENCESLAS
QUEEN ROSAMUND
BOLESLAS ⎫
LADISLAS ⎬ their sons
BOGGERLAS ⎭
GENERAL LASKI
STANISLAS LESZCZYNSKI
JOHN SOBIESKI III
NICOLAS RENSKI
THE TSAR ALEXIS
GYRON ⎫
HEADS ⎬ Palcontents
TAILS ⎭
CONSPIRATORS and
  SOLDIERS

PEOPLE
MICHAEL FEODOROVITCH
NOBLES
JUDGES
COUNSELLORS
FINANCIERS
LACKEYS OF THE PHYNAN-
  CES
PEASANTS
THE ENTIRE RUSSIAN ARMY
THE ENTIRE POLISH ARMY
MA UBU'S GUARDS
A CAPTAIN
THE BEAR
THE PHYNANCE CHARGER
THE DEBRAINING MACHINE
THE CREW
THE SEA-CAPTAIN

The play was originally presented by Lugné-Poe and the
Théâtre de l'Œuvre at the Salle du Nouveau Théâtre on
December 10th, 1896. The direction was by Lugné-Poe with
décor by Paul Sérusier, masks by Alfred Jarry and music by
Claude Terrasse.

The cast included Firmin Gémier as Père Ubu and Louise
France as Mère Ubu.

Act One

SCENE ONE

PA UBU, MA UBU

PA UBU. Pschitt!

MA UBU. Ooh! what a nasty word. Pa Ubu, you're a dirty old man.

PA UBU. Watch out I don't bash yer nut in, Ma Ubu!

MA UBU. It's not me you should want to do in, Old Ubu. Oh, no! There's someone else for the high jump.

PA UBU. By my green candle, I'm not with you.

MA UBU. How come, Old Ubu, you mean you're content with your lot?

PA UBU. By my green candle, pschitt, Madam. Yes, by God, I'm perfectly satisfied. Who wouldn't be? Captain of the Dragoons, aide de camp to King Wenceslas, decorated with the order of the Red Eagle of Poland, and ex-King of Aragon. You can't go higher than that!

MA UBU. So what! After having been King of Aragon, you're content to ride in reviews at the head of fifty bumpkins armed with billhooks when you could get your loaf measured for the crown of Poland?

PA UBU. Huh? I don't understand a word you're saying, Mother.

MA UBU. How stupid can you get!

PA UBU. By my green candle, King Wenceslas is still alive, isn't he? And even if he does kick the bucket, hasn't he masses of children?

MA UBU. Why shouldn't you finish off the whole bunch and put yourself in their place?

PA UBU. Ha! Madam, now you have gone too far, and you shall very shortly be beaten up good and proper.

MA UBU. You poor slob, if I get beaten up who'll patch the seat of your pants?

PA UBU. So what! Haven't I a bum like everyone else?

MA UBU. If I were you, I'd try to get that bum sitting on a throne. You could become enormously rich, eat as many bangers as you liked, and roll through the streets in a fine carriage.

PA UBU. If I were king, I'd get them to make me a great bonnet like the one I used to wear in Aragon, which those lousy Spaniards had the nerve to pinch off me.

MA UBU. And you could get yourself an umbrella and a guards officer's greatcoat that would come down to your feet.

PA UBU. It is more than I can resist! Pschittabugger and buggerapschitt, if ever I come across him alone on a dark night, he's for it.

MA UBU. Well done, Pa Ubu, now you're talking like a man.

PA UBU. Oh no! Me – a captain of dragoons – brutally murder the King of Poland! I would rather die!

MA UBU (aside). Oh, pschitt! (Aloud.) So you want to stay poor as a church mouse, Mister Ubu?

PA UBU. God's bones, yes, by my green candle, I'd rather be poor as the skinniest mouse than rich as the cruellest cat.

MA UBU. And your bonnet? And your umbrella? And your greatcoat?

PA UBU. And then what, you old cow?

He leaves, banging the door behind him.

MA UBU (alone). Pfartt, pschitt, what a stingy bastard, but pfartt, pschitt, I think I've got him shifting all the same. Thanks be to God and myself, in a week, perhaps, I may be Queen of Poland.

SCENE TWO

A room in PA UBU's *house, where a magnificent collation is set out.*

PA UBU, MA UBU

MA UBU. Well, our guests are pretty late.

PA UBU. Yes, by my green candle, I'm dying of hunger. You're looking exceptionally ugly tonight, Madam, is it because we have company?

MA UBU (*shrugging her shoulders*). Pschitt.

PA UBU (*seizing a roast chicken*). I'm quite hungry. I think I'll get my teeth into this bird. Hmm, a chicken, I reckon, and not bad at all.

MA UBU. Stop it, you wretch! What are our guests going to eat?

PA UBU. There'll still be plenty for them. I shan't touch another thing. Go and look out of the window, Ma Ubu, and see if our guests are arriving.

MA UBU (*going over*). I don't see a soul.

Meanwhile, PA UBU *gets his hands on a fillet of veal.*

MA UBU. Ah, here comes Captain M'Nure and his merry men. Hey, Old Ubu, what are you eating?

PA UBU. Nothing, nothing. Just a spot of veal.

MA UBU. Oh, my veal, my veal! The lout! He's eaten the veal! Help! Help!

PA UBU. By my green candle, I'll gouge your eyes out.

The door opens.

SCENE THREE

PA UBU, MA UBU, CAPTAIN MACNURE *and his* MERRY MEN

MA UBU. Good day, gentlemen, we have been awaiting your arrival with impatience. Pray be seated.

CAPTAIN MACNURE. Good day, Madam. But where is Mister Ubu?

PA UBU. Here I am, here I am! By my green candle, dammit, I shouldn't have thought I was so easy to miss.

CAPTAIN MACNURE. Good day, Mister Ubu. Sit ye down, my merry men.

They all sit down.

PA UBU. Ouch! A little more grub and my chair would have collapsed.

CAPTAIN MACNURE. Well, Mistress Ubu, what succulent dishes have you prepared for us today?

MA UBU. Here's the menu.

PA UBU. That's right up my street.

MA UBU. Polish broth, spare ribs of Polish bison, veal, chicken
and hound pie, parsons' noses from the royal Polish turkeys,
charlotte russe . . .

PA UBU. That's enough, I should think. Is there any more?

MA UBU. Ice-pudding, salad, fruit, cheese, boiled beef,
Jerusalem fartichokes, cauliflower à la pschitt.

PA UBU. Hey, do you think I'm an oriental potentate, shelling
out all that money?

MA UBU. Pay no attention to him. He's off his rocker.

PA UBU. You wait. I shall sharpen my teeth on your shanks.

MA UBU. Just eat up and shut up, Old Ubu! Here, try the
Polish broth.

PA UBU. Urghh, what muck!

CAPTAIN MACNURE. You're right. It hasn't quite come off.

MA UBU. Ill-mannered louts, what do you want then?

PA UBU (*clapping his brow*). Ah! I've got an idea. Back in a
jiffy.

He goes out.

MA UBU. Gentlemen, let's try the veal.

CAPTAIN MACNURE. Excellent. What there was of it.

MA UBU. Now for the parsons' noses.

CAPTAIN MACNURE. Absolutely delicious. Hurrah for Ma
Ubu!

ALL. Hurrah for Ma Ubu.

PA UBU (*returning*). And soon you'll be yelling hurrah for Old
Ubu.

*He holds an unmentionable brush in his hand and hurls it at the
gathering.*

PA UBU. Try a taste of that. (*Several taste and collapse poisoned.*)
Now pass me the spare ribs of Polish bison, Mother, and I'll
dish them out.

MA UBU. Here they are.

PA UBU. Get out everybody! I have something to say to you,
Captain M'Nure.

THE REST. But we haven't had our dinner!

PA UBU. Not had dinner? Get out, I tell you. Not you, M'Nure. (*Nobody budges.*) You're still here? By my green candle, I'll do you all in with bison ribs.

He begins to throw them.

ALL. Ooh! Ow! Help, rescue! Let's stick up for ourselves! Curses! He's done for me!

PA UBU. Pschitt, pschitt and pschitt again. Get out, all of you. Do I make myself plain?

ALL. Every man for himself! Rotten old Ubu! Mean, double-crossing skunk!

PA UBU. Ah, they've gone. Now I can relax again, but I've had a lousy meal. Come, M'Nure.

They leave with MA UBU.

SCENE FOUR

PA UBU, MA UBU, CAPTAIN MACNURE

PA UBU. Well, captain, how did you enjoy your dinner?

CAPTAIN MACNURE. Very much, Sir, except for the pschitt.

PA UBU. Oh, I didn't think the pschitt was too bad.

MA UBU. A little of what you fancy, they say.

PA UBU. Captain M'Nure, I've decided to create you Duke of Lithuania.

CAPTAIN MACNURE. But I thought you were completely broke, Mister Ubu?

PA UBU. In a day or two, with your help, I shall be King of Poland.

CAPTAIN MACNURE. You will assassinate Wenceslas?

PA UBU. The bugger's no fool. He's guessed it.

CAPTAIN MACNURE. If it's a question of killing Wenceslas, I'm with you. I am his deadly enemy, and I can answer for my men.

PA UBU (*throwing himself upon him to embrace him*). Oh, M'Nure, I love you dearly for that.

CAPTAIN MACNURE. Pooh, how you stink, man! Don't you ever wash?

PA UBU. Occasionally.

MA UBU. Never!

PA UBU. I'm going to tread on your toes.

MA UBU. Fat lump of pschitt!

PA UBU. Right, M'Nure, that's all for now. But by my green candle, I swear on the head of Madam Ubu to make you Duke of Lithuania.

MA UBU. But . . .

PA UBU. Silence, my angel . . .

They all go out.

SCENE FIVE

PA UBU, MA UBU, A MESSENGER

PA UBU. What do you want, Sir? Piss off. You make me sick and tired.

MESSENGER. Sir, you are summoned immediately to the royal presence.

He goes out.

PA UBU. Oh pschitt! God's whiskers! By my green candle, all is discovered. I'll be beheaded. Woe is me!

MA UBU. What a feeble creature! And time's getting short.

PA UBU. Ah! I've got an idea. I'll say it was Ma Ubu and M'Nure.

MA UBU. You big P.U., you just try . . .

PA UBU. I'd better get out while the going's good.

He goes out.

MA UBU (*running after him*). Oh! Pa Ubu, Pa Ubu, I'll give you some fine fat sausages.

She goes out.

PA UBU (*offstage*). Oh pschitt! You're a fine fat sausage yourself.

SCENE SIX

The King's Palace

KING WENCESLAS, *surrounded by his* OFFICERS; MAC-
NURE; THE KING'S SONS, BOLESLAS, LADISLAS
and BOGGERLAS

PA UBU (*entering*). Oh! you know, it wasn't me, it was the old
woman and M'Nure.

THE KING. What's up with you, Old Ubu?

CAPTAIN MACNURE. He's tight.

THE KING. Like me this morning. I was tight as two Poles.

PA UBU. Yes, I'm tight. It's because I've drunk too much
champagne.

THE KING. Master Ubu, I have resolved to reward you for
your many services as Captain of Dragoons, and I therefore
proclaim you Count of Sandomir.

PA UBU. O, Sire! I am speechless with gratitude.

THE KING. Tut, think nothing of it, Master Ubu. But be sure
to be present tomorrow morning at our Grand Review.

PA UBU. I shall be there, Sire. Meanwhile, pray deign to
accept this magnificently decorated kazoo.

He presents the KING *with a kazoo.*

THE KING. You don't expect me to start playing a kazoo at my
age, surely? Well, I'll give it to young Boggerlas.

BOGGERLAS. What an old fool he is, this Ubu creature.

PA UBU. And now I shall fuck off. (*He falls, as he turns round.*)
Oh! ow! Help, rescue! By my green candle, I've ruptured
my gut and smashed my rattle-trap.

THE KING (*helping him up*). Old Ubu, are you hurt?

PA UBU. Yes, badly, and I'm certainly going to croak. What
will happen to Madam Ubu?

THE KING. We shall provide for her upkeep.

PA UBU. You are most kind and gracious, Sire. (*Aside, as he
leaves.*) But you'll be liquidated just the same, King
Wenceslas.

SCENE SEVEN

Ubu's House

GYRON, HEADS, TAILS, PA UBU, MA UBU, CONSPIRATORS
and SOLDIERS, CAPTAIN MACNURE

PA UBU. Well, my good friends, it's high time we planned our
little conspiracy. Let each give his counsel. With your permission, we will begin with mine.

CAPTAIN MACNURE. Speak, Mister Ubu.

PA UBU. Very good, my friends. I'm of the opinion that we
should simply poison the King by stuffing his lunch with
arsenic. When he starts the browsing and scoffing, he'll drop
dead, and I shall be king.

ALL. Oo, you wicked old thing, you!

PA UBU. What, you don't like that idea? All right then, let's
hear from M'Nure.

CAPTAIN MACNURE. My suggestion is that I fetch him a good
wallop with my sword and cleave him from top to toe.

ALL. Ah yes! that's noble and gallant.

PA UBU. But supposing he gives you a few kicks? I've just
remembered: for his Grand Reviews, he wears iron boots
that are jolly painful. If I had half a chance, I'd snitch on the
lot of you. That way, I'd be rid of this whole beastly business, and probably pick up a reward into the bargain.

MA UBU. Oh, the traitor, the coward, the rotten, mean skunk!

ALL. Down with Old Ubu!

PA UBU. Hey, gentlemen, shut your traps unless you want me
to turn you all in. Well, all right, then, I'll take all the risks
on your behalf. So, M'Nure, it's agreed that your job is to
split the king down the middle.

CAPTAIN MACNURE. Wouldn't it be better for us all to jump
on him at once, shouting and yelling? That way, we'd have
a better chance of winning over the troops.

PA UBU. Look, I'll tell you what. I shall try to step on his toe,
he'll kick out at me, I'll say 'PSCHITT' to him, and that
will be the signal for you all to hurl yourselves on him.

MA UBU. Yes, and the moment he's dead, you'll take his crown and sceptre.

CAPTAIN MACNURE. And I and my men will go in pursuit of the royal family.

PA UBU. Yes, and keep a special look-out for young Boggerlas.

They go out.
PA UBU *runs after them and makes them come back.*

Gentlemen, we have forgotten an indispensable ceremony. We must take an oath to quit ourselves like men.

CAPTAIN MACNURE. How can we? We haven't got a priest.

PA UBU. My old woman will act as priest.

ALL. All right, so be it.

PA UBU. And so you all swear to kill the King good and proper?

ALL. We swear it. Long live Old Ubu!

Act Two

SCENE ONE

The King's Palace

WENCESLAS, QUEEN ROSAMUND, BOLESLAS, LADISLAS and
BOGGERLAS

THE KING. Prince Boggerlas, you were extremely cheeky this
morning to Master Ubu, Knight of my Orders and Count of
Sandomir. Therefore I forbid you to appear at our Grand
Review.

THE QUEEN. But, Wenceslas, you will need every single member of your family around you to protect you vigilantly
today.

THE KING. Madam, I never take back what I've said. You
bore me with your idle chatter.

BOGGERLAS. My royal father, I submit.

THE QUEEN. Really, Sire, are you quite determined to attend
this Parade?

THE KING. Pray, Madam, why not?

THE QUEEN. I'll tell you once more. I saw him in a dream,
smiting you with massed weapons and throwing you into
the Vistula, and an eagle like that which figures in the Arms
of Poland placing the crown on his head.

THE KING. Whose head?

THE QUEEN. Old Ubu's.

THE KING. Ridiculous! The Lord Ubu is a most worthy
gentleman who would let himself be dragged apart by wild
horses rather than betray my interests.

THE QUEEN *and* BOGGERLAS (*together*). How wrong you
are!

THE KING. Silence, young rascal. And as for you, Madam, to
show you what complete confidence I have in Master Ubu,
I shall attend the Grand Review as I am, without sword and
breastplate.

THE QUEEN. What fatal rashness! I shall never see you again alive.

THE KING. Come, Ladislas. Come, Boleslas.

They go out. THE QUEEN *and* BOGGERLAS *go to the window.*

THE QUEEN *and* BOGGERLAS (*together*). May God and the great Saint Nicholas protect you!

THE QUEEN. Boggerlas, accompany me to the chapel to pray for your father and your brothers.

SCENE TWO

The Parade Ground

THE POLISH ARMY, THE KING, BOLESLAS, LADISLAS, PA UBU, CAPTAIN MACNURE and his MERRY MEN, GYRON, HEADS, TAILS

THE KING. Noble Master Ubu, enter the royal enclosure with your followers, and we will review the march past together.

PA UBU (*to his* HENCHMEN). Look sharp, you clots. (*To* THE KING.) Coming, Sire, coming.

UBU'S MEN *surround* THE KING.

THE KING. Ah, there's my regiment of Danziger Horseguards. What a magnificent spectacle!

PA UBU. You think so? They look to me like something the cat brought in. Look at that one! (*Pointing to a soldier.*) How many days since you last had a shave, you lousy scum?

THE KING. But this soldier is very well turned out. What on earth is the matter with you, Old Ubu?

PA UBU. This! (*He stamps on* THE KING'S *foot.*)

THE KING. Treason!

PA UBU. PSCHITT. Rally round me, my fine fellows.

CAPTAIN MACNURE. Up guards and at him! Hurrah!

All strike THE KING. *A* PALCONTENT *explodes.*

THE KING. Help, help! Holy Virgin, I'm dying.

BOLESLAS (*to* LADISLAS). What's going on? Have at them!

PA UBU. Ha! I have the crown. Now for the others.
CAPTAIN MACNURE. Death to the traitors!

THE KING'S SONS *flee. All pursue them.*

SCENE THREE

THE QUEEN *and* BOGGERLAS

THE QUEEN. At last I begin to feel reassured.
BOGGERLAS. You have nothing to be afraid of. (*A fearful din is heard outside.*) Oh no! What do I see? My two brothers pursued by Old Ubu and his men.
THE QUEEN. Oh God! Holy Virgin, they are losing ground.
BOGGERLAS. The whole army is following Ubu. The King is no longer there. It's horrible. Help, help!
THE QUEEN. Now Boleslas is dead! Struck by a fatal bullet.
BOGGERLAS. Ho there! (LADISLAS *turns round.*) Defend yourself. Bravo, Ladislas!
THE QUEEN. Oh! he's surrounded.
BOGGERLAS. He's done for. M'Nure has just split him in two like a sausage.
THE QUEEN. Help, help! Those maniacs have forced their way into the palace. They're coming up the stairs.

The din grows louder.

THE QUEEN
BOGGERLAS } (*on their knees*). May God protect us!
BOGGERLAS. Oh, that vile Ubu, wretch, rascal, I'd just like to get hold of him . . .

SCENE FOUR

The same. The door is broken in. PA UBU *enters, followed by his mob of* LUNATICS.

PA UBU. Oh, you would, would you, Boggerlas? And what, pray would you do to me?

BOGGERLAS. By God's will, I shall defend my mother to the death. The first man to take a step forward is as good as dead.
PA UBU. M'Nure, I'm scared. Get me out of here.
A SOLDIER (*advances*). Boggerlas, surrender.
BOGGERLAS. Here's one for you, you dog! (*He splits his skull*).
THE QUEEN. That's the spirit, Boggerlas, keep it up!
SEVERAL (*advancing*). Boggerlas, we promise to save your life.
BOGGERLAS. Blackguards, wine-bladders, mercenary scum.

He flourishes his sword and massacres the lot of them.

PA UBU. Bother! But I'll still win in the end.
BOGGERLAS. Mother, escape by the secret staircase.
THE QUEEN. And you, my son, what about you?
BOGGERLAS. I'll follow you.
PA UBU. Quick. Capture the Queen. Drat, she's got away. As for you, you little worm! . . . (*He advances on* BOGGERLAS.)
BOGGERLAS. Ah! by God's will, here's my vengeance!

He rips open PA UBU's *boodle with a terrible sword-thrust.*

Mother, I follow you!

He disappears by the secret staircase.

SCENE FIVE

A cavern in the mountains.

BOGGERLAS *enters, followed by* QUEEN ROSAMUND.

BOGGERLAS. Here we shall be safe.
THE QUEEN. Oh, I do hope so. Boggerlas, support me!

She falls on the snow.

BOGGERLAS. What ails you, mother dear?
THE QUEEN. I am sick unto death, Boggerlas, and fear I have only a few hours to live.
BOGGERLAS. What! have you caught a chill?
THE QUEEN. How do you think I can stand up to so many misfortunes? The King murdered, our family destroyed, and you, a scion of the noblest race that ever carried a sword,

forced to flee to the mountains like a common smuggler?

BOGGERLAS. And by whom, great God, by whom? A vulgar wretch like Ubu, a common little adventurer, a mister nobody from nowhere, fat toad, stinking tramp! And when I think that my father decorated him and made him a count, and the very next day that villain shamelessly laid violent hands on him.

THE QUEEN. O Boggerlas! When I think how happy we all were before that wicked old Ubu arrived on the scene. But now, alas, everything is changed.

BOGGERLAS. What can we do, but wait in hope and never renounce our rights?

THE QUEEN. I long for your just restitution, my dear child, but I fear that I myself shall never see that happy day.

BOGGERLAS. Here, what's come over you? She grows pale, she swoons! Help, help! But we are alone in the wilderness! My God, her heart has stopped beating. She is dead. Can it be possible? Yet another victim of the fiendish Ubu!

He buries his face in his hands and weeps.

Ah God, how tragic to find oneself all alone at the age of fourteen with a terrible vengeance to pursue!

He falls prey to the most violent despair.
Meanwhile, the SOULS *of* WENCESLAS, BOLESLAS, LADISLAS *and* ROSAMUND *enter the cavern. The oldest of them approaches* BOGGERLAS *and rouses him gently from his stupor.*

BOGGERLAS. Ah! What do I see? My whole family, my ancestors . . . What miracle is this?

THE SHADE. Learn, Boggerlas, that during my lifetime I was Lord Mathias of Königsberg, the first king – and founder – of our House. I leave our vengeance in your hands. (*He presents him with an enormous sword.*) And may this sword which I present to you know no rest until it shall have dealt death to the usurper.

All vanish, and BOGGERLAS *remains alone in an attitude of ecstasy.*

SCENE SIX

The King's Palace

PA UBU, MA UBU, CAPTAIN MACNURE

PA UBU. No! nothing doing, I say! Do you want to ruin me just for these buffoons?

CAPTAIN MACNURE. But look here, Old Ubu, don't you see that your people are expecting gifts to celebrate your glorious coronation?

MA UBU. If you don't give them a great feast and plenty of gold, you'll be overthrown in a couple of hours.

PA UBU. A feast, yes, but money, never! Slaughter three old nags, that's quite good enough for such scum.

MA UBU. Scum yourself! How did such a crummy creature as you ever get slapped together?

PA UBU. Do I have to repeat myself? I intend to get rich, I won't fork out a penny.

MA UBU. Don't forget you hold in your hands all the treasure of Poland!

CAPTAIN MACNURE. Yes, I know where there's a vast hoard hidden in the chapel; let's distribute that.

PA UBU. Just you try that on, you wretch.

CAPTAIN MACNURE. Listen, Old Ubu, if you don't distribute some money, no one will want to pay their taxes.

PA UBU. Is that really true?

MA UBU. Yes, yes!

PA UBU. Oh, in that case, I agree to everything. Bring up two or three million gold pieces, roast a hundred and fifty oxen and the same number of sheep, and see that there's plenty left over for me.

They go out.

SCENE SEVEN

The Courtyard of the Palace, full of People

PA UBU, *crowned*, MA UBU, CAPTAIN MACNURE, LACKEYS *loaded with dishes of roast meat.*

PEOPLE. There's the King! Long live the King! Hurrah!

PA UBU (*throwing gold*). Here, you, catch. Don't thank me. All this throwing gold away is no pleasure to me at all, but my old woman insisted. At least, promise you'll pay your taxes now.

ALL. Yes, yes!

CAPTAIN MACNURE. Just look, Madam Ubu, how they are fighting over the gold. What a battle!

MA UBU. Perfectly dreadful! Ugh! there's one who's had his skull bashed in.

PA UBU. What a beautiful sight! Bring up more chests of gold.

CAPTAIN MACNURE. How about organizing a race?

PA UBU. Yes, that's an idea. (*To the* PEOPLE.) My friends, you see this chest full of gold? It contains three hundred thousand rose-nobles in gold, all genuine Polish coin of the realm. Those who want to run in the race go to the end of the courtyard. You start running when I wave my handker-chief, and the winner gets the chest. And for the losers, there's this second chest of gold to share out as a booby prize.

ALL. Yes! Long live Old Ubu! What a decent King! We never had fun like this during the reign of Wenceslas.

PA UBU (*to* MA UBU, *joyfully*). Just listen to them!

All the PEOPLE *line up at the far end of the courtyard.*

PA UBU. One, two, three! Are you ready?

ALL. Yes! Yes!

PA UBU. Go!

They start running. Tripping, tumbling and falling over each other. Cries and tumult.

CAPTAIN MACNURE. They're coming! They're coming!

PA UBU. Ha! The one in front is losing ground.

MA UBU. No, he's ahead again.

CAPTAIN MACNURE. Oh! he's losing, he's losing! All over! It's the other one.

The one who had been second finishes first.

ALL. Long live Michael Federovitch! Long live Michael
Federovitch!

MICHAEL FEDEROVITCH. Sire, I really don't know how to
thank Your Majesty . . .

PA UBU. Oh, my dear friend, it's nothing. Take that chest
home with you, Michael. And the rest of you share the
other chest: each take a gold piece until there are none left.

ALL. Long live Michael Federovitch! Long live Old Ubu!

PA UBU. All of you, my friends, come and dine with me. The
gates of my palace are open to you today, please honour me
with your presence at table.

PEOPLE. In we go! In we go! Long live Old Ubu! The
noblest of all monarchs!

*They enter the Palace. The noise of the orgy, which lasts till the
following day, can be heard. The curtain falls.*

Act Three

SCENE ONE

The Palace

PA UBU, MA UBU

PA UBU. By my green candle, behold me, monarch of this fair land. I've already got the gut-ache from overeating, and soon they are going to bring in my great bonnet.

MA UBU. What's it made of, my beloved lord and master? Because, even though we are now King and Queen, we've still got to be economical.

PA UBU. Madam my female, it's of sheepskin, with a clasp and tie-strings of doghide.

MA UBU. That sounds pretty good, but royalty's even better.

PA UBU. Yes, you were right as usual, Ma Ubu.

MA UBU. We owe a great debt of gratitude to the Duke of Lithuania.

PA UBU. Who's that?

MA UBU. Why, Captain M'Nure.

PA UBU. For heaven's sake, woman, don't even mention that slob to me. Now that I don't need him any more, he can whistle for his dukedom, because he certainly won't get it.

MA UBU. You're making a big mistake, Old Ubu. He'll turn against you.

PA UBU. I should worry! As far as I'm concerned, he and Boggerlas can go jump in a lake.

MA UBU. And do you think you've heard the last of Boggerlas?

PA UBU. Sword of phynance, obviously! What harm do you think he can do me, that little fourteen-year-old squirt?

MA UBU. Just you mark my words, Pa Ubu. You should try to win over Boggerlas to you by your generosity.

PA UBU. More money to dish out? Not on your life! You've already made me pour at least two millions down the drain.

MA UBU. Have it your own way, Old Ubu. But I warn you, he'll settle your hash.

PA UBU. Then you'll find yourself in the same stewpot with me.

MA UBU. For the last time, I warn you. Young Boggerlas may very well carry the day. After all, he has justice on his side.

PA UBU. Oh, tripe! Isn't injustice just as good as justice? Ah! you're taking the piss out of me, Madam, I'm going to chop you into tiny pieces.

MA UBU *flees for her life, pursued by* PA UBU.

SCENE TWO

The Great Hall of the Palace.

PA UBU, MA UBU, OFFICERS *and* SOLDIERS: GYRON, HEADS, TAILS; NOBLES *in chains,* FINANCIERS, JUDGES, REGISTRARS.

PA UBU. Bring out the chest for Nobles, and the boat-hook for Nobles, and the slasher for Nobles and the account book for Nobles, and then – bring in the Nobles.

The NOBLES *are brutally shoved in.*

MA UBU. For pity's sake restrain yourself, Old Ubu.

PA UBU. My lords, I have the honour to inform you that as a gesture to the economic welfare of my kingdom, I have resolved to liquidate the entire nobility and confiscate their goods.

NOBLES. Horror of horrors! Soldiers and citizens, defend us.

PA UBU. Bring up the first Noble and pass me the boat-hook. Those who are condemned to death, I shall push through this trap door. They will fall down into the bleed-pig chambers, and will then proceed to the cash-room where they will be debrained. (*To the* NOBLE.) What's your name, you slob?

NOBLE. Count of Vitebsk.

PA UBU. What's your income?

NOBLE. Three million rix-dollars.

PA UBU. Guilty. (*He grabs him with the hook and pushes him down the hole.*)

MA UBU. What base brutality!

PA UBU. You, there, what's your name? (*The* NOBLE *doesn't answer.*) Go on – answer, you slob.

NOBLE. Grand Duke of Posen.

PA UBU. Excellent! Excellent! I couldn't ask for a better. Down the hatch. Next one. What's your name, ugly mug?

NOBLE. Duke of Courland, and of the cities of Riga, Revel and Mitau.

PA UBU. Very good indeed. Sure that's the lot?

NOBLE. That's all.

PA UBU. Down the hatch, then. Number four, what's your name?

NOBLE. Prince of Podolia.

PA UBU. Income?

NOBLE. I'm bankrupt.

PA UBU. Take that for disrespect. (*Hits him with the hook.*) Now get down that hatch. Your name, number five?

NOBLE. Margrave of Thorn, Count Palatine of Polock.

PA UBU. That's not much. Is that all you are?

NOBLE. It's been good enough for me.

PA UBU. Well, it's better than nothing. Down the hatch. What's eating you, Ma Ubu?

MA UBU. You're too bloodthirsty, Pa Ubu.

PA UBU. Bah! I'm getting rich. Now I'll have them read the list of what *I've* got. Registrar, read *my* list of *my* titles and possessions.

REGISTRAR. Count of Sandomir.

PA UBU. Begin with the princedoms, stupid bugger!

REGISTRAR. Princedom of Podolia, Grand Duchy of Posen, Duchy of Courland, County of Sandomir, County of Vitebsk, Palatinate of Polock, Margravate of Thorn.

PA UBU. Well, go on.

REGISTRAR. That's the lot.

PA UBU. What do you mean, that's the lot! Oh well, then, forward all the Nobles and, since I don't propose to stop getting richer, I shall execute them all and confiscate their revenues. Come on, down the hatch with the whole lot. (*They are stuffed down the hatch.*) Hurry up, faster, faster, I'm going to make some laws next.

SEVERAL. That'll be worth watching.

PA UBU. First of all, I shall reform the code of justice, then we will proceed to financial matters.

SEVERAL JUDGES. We are strongly opposed to any change.

PA UBU. Pschitt! Firstly, judges will no longer receive a salary.

JUDGES. And what shall we live on? We're all poor men.

PA UBU. You can keep the fines you impose and the possessions of those you condemn to death.

FIRST JUDGE. It's unthinkable.

SECOND JUDGE. Infamous.

THIRD JUDGE. Scandalous.

FOURTH JUDGE. Contemptible.

ALL. We refuse to judge under such conditions.

PA UBU. Down the hatch with the judges. (*They struggle in vain.*)

MA UBU. Oh, what have you done, Pa Ubu? Who will administer justice now?

PA UBU. Why, I will. You'll see how well things will go.

MA UBU. Yes, it will be a right old mess.

PA UBU. Aw, shut your gob, clownish female. Gentlemen, we will proceed to financial matters.

FINANCIERS. There's no need to change anything.

PA UBU. How come? I wish to change everything, I do. To begin with, I intend to pocket half the tax receipts.

FINANCIERS. What a cheek!

PA UBU. Gentlemen, we shall establish a tax of ten percent on all property, another on industry, and a third of fifteen francs a head on all marriages and funerals.

FIRST FINANCIER. But that's ridiculous, Pa Ubu.

SECOND FINANCIER. Quite absurd.

THIRD FINANCIER. Doesn't make sense.

PA UBU. You're making fun of me? Down the hatch, all of you. (*The* FINANCIERS *are shoved in.*)

MA UBU. Come, come, Lord Ubu, kings aren't supposed to behave like that. You're butchering the whole world.

PA UBU. So pschitt!

MA UBU. No more justice, no financial system!

PA UBU. Fear nothing, my sweet child, I'll go from village to village myself and collect the taxes.

SCENE THREE

A Peasant's House in the Environs of Warsaw.

Several PEASANTS *are assembled.*

A PEASANT (*entering*). Hey! did you hear the news? The King is dead, and all the nobles as well; young Boggerlas has fled to the mountains with his mother. What's more, Pa Ubu has seized the throne.

ANOTHER. Yes, and here's something else. I've just come from Cracow, where I saw them carting off the bodies of more than three hundred nobles and five hundred magistrates that he's had slaughtered, and it seems they're going to double the taxes and that Pa Ubu is going to make the rounds in person to collect them.

ALL. Great God! What will become of us? Pa Ubu is a foul beast and they say that his whole family is equally repulsive.

A PEASANT. Hark! It sounds like someone's knocking at the door.

A VOICE (*off*). Hornstrumpot! Open up, pschitt, in the names of St John, St Peter and St Nicolas! Open up, by my cash-sword and my cash-horn, I've come to collect the taxes!

The door is smashed in. UBU *enters, followed by an army of money-grubbers.*

SCENE FOUR

PA UBU. Which of you is the oldest? (*A* PEASANT *steps forward.*) What's your name?

PEASANT. Stanislas Leczinski.

PA UBU. Well then, hornstrumpot, listen carefully, or these gentlemen will extrude your nearoles. Hey, listen, will you!

STANISLAS. But Your Excellency hasn't said anything yet.

PA UBU. What! I've been talking for an hour. Do you think I came here simply to amuse myself with the echo of my own voice?

STANISLAS: No thought could be farther from my mind, Sire.

PA UBU. All right, then. I've come to tell you, order you, and inform you that you are to produce and display your ready cash immediately, or you'll be massacred. Come on in, my lords of phynance, you sons of whores, wheel in the phynancial wheelbarrow.

The wheelbarrow is wheeled in.

STANISLAS. Sire, we are down on the register for only one hundred and fifty-two rix-dollars, which we've already paid over six weeks ago come Michaelmas.

PA UBU. That may well be so, but I've changed the government and I've had it announced in the official gazette that all the present taxes have to be paid twice over, and all those I may think up later on will have to be paid three times over. With this system, I'll soon make a fortune: then I'll kill everyone in the world, and go away.

PEASANTS. Mercy, Lord Ubu, have pity on us. We are poor, simple people.

PA UBU. I couldn't care less. Pay up.

PEASANTS. But we can't, we've already paid.

PA UBU. Fork out! Or I'll give you the works good and proper: torture, twisting of the neck, and decapitation. Hornstrumpot, am I or am I not your King?

ALL. Ho, in that case, to arms, fellows! Long live Boggerlas, by the grace of God King of Poland and Lithuania!

PA UBU. Advance, gentlemen of the Phynances, do your duty.

A fight takes place. The house is razed to the ground, and only old STANISLAS *escapes and flees alone across the plain.* UBU *stays behind to scoop up the cash.*

SCENE FIVE

A casemate in the fortifications of Thorn. MACNURE *in chains,* PA UBU.

PA UBU. Well, citizen, you're in a fine pickle, aren't you? You
wanted me to pay you what I owed you, and when I refused
to you rebelled and plotted against me, and where did that
land you? In jug! Hornboodle, the clever trick I played on
you was so mean it should be right up your street.

MACNURE. Take care, treacherous old Ubu. In the five days
you've been King you've committed more crimes and
murders than it would take to damn all the saints in Paradise.
The blood of the King and the Nobles cries for vengeance,
and those cries will be heard.

PA UBU. Ha, my fine friend, you've got a glib tongue, all right,
and I don't doubt that if you should escape you might make
things difficult for me. But, to the best of my knowledge,
the casemates of Thorn have never released from their
clutches any of the fine fellows entrusted to their tender
care. So, good night to you, and sleep tight if you can,
though I should warn you that the rats here go through a
very pretty routine at night.

He goes out. The TURNKEYS *arrive and lock and bolt all the
doors.*

SCENE SIX

The Palace in Moscow.

THE TSAR ALEXIS *and his court,* MACNURE.

ALEXIS. So it was you, base soldier of fortune, who took part
in the assassination of our cousin Wenceslas?

MACNURE. Sire, grant me your royal pardon. I was dragged
into the plot by Old Ubu, despite myself.

ALEXIS. Oh, what a bare-faced liar! Well, what do you want?

MACNURE. Old Ubu accused me falsely of conspiracy and had
me thrown in gaol. I managed to escape and have been
spurring my horse for five days and nights across the steppes
to come and plead for your gracious mercy.

ALEXIS. What can you show me as practical proof of your
loyalty?

MACNURE. The sword I wielded as a soldier of fortune, and a detailed map of the fortified city of Thorn.

ALEXIS. I accept the sword as a symbol of your submission, but by St George, burn the map. I don't intend to achieve my victory through treachery.

MACNURE. One of the sons of Wenceslas, young Boggerlas, is still alive. I would do anything in my power to help restore him to the throne.

ALEXIS. What was your rank in the Polish army?

MACNURE. I commanded the fifth regiment of Vilna dragoons and a company of mercenaries in the service of Captain Ubu.

ALEXIS. Good. I appoint you second lieutenant in the tenth Cossack regiment, and woe betide you if you betray me. If you fight well, you shall be rewarded.

MACNURE. Courage I have in plenty, Sire.

ALEXIS. Good. Remove yourself from my presence.

He leaves.

SCENE SEVEN

UBU's *council chamber.*

PA UBU, MA UBU, PHYNANCIAL COUNSELLORS.

PA UBU. Gentlemen, I declare this meeting open. Try to keep your ears open and your mouths shut. First, we shall deal with finance, and then we shall discuss a little system I've thought up for bringing fine weather and keeping rain away.

A COUNSELLOR. Splendid, Mister Ubu, Sir.

MA UBU. What a numbskull.

PA UBU. Madam of my pschitt, look out, I'm not going to stand any more of your nonsense. As I was about to say to you, gentlemen, our finances are in a fairly good state. A considerable number of our hirelings clutching well-filled stockings prowl the streets every morning and the sons of whores are doing fine. In all directions there is a vista of burning houses and the sight of our peoples groaning under the weight of our phynance.

SAME COUNSELLOR. And how are the new taxes going, Mister Ubu, sir?

MA UBU. Not at all well. The tax on marriages has only produced eleven pence so far, even though Mister Ubu's been chasing people all over the place to force them to marry.

PA UBU. Sword of phynance, horn of my strumpot, madam financieress, I have nearoles to speak with and you have a mouth to listen to me with. (*Bursts of laughter.*) No, no, that's not what I meant to say! You're always getting me mixed up, yes, it's your fault I'm so stupid! But, by the horn of Ubu! ... (*A* MESSENGER *enters.*) Now what does this fellow want? Get out, oaf, before I black both your eyes, cut your head off and make corkscrews out of your legs.

MA UBU. He's gone already, but he's left a letter.

PA UBU. Read it. I don't know, I'm either going out of my mind or I've forgotten how to read. Hurry up, clownish female, it's probably from M'Nure.

MA UBU. Exactly. He says that the Tsar has welcomed him most graciously, that he's going to invade your Territories to restore Boggerlas to the throne and that you'll certainly end up swinging at the end of a rope.

PA UBU. Hooh! Hah! I'm scared! Ooh, I'm frightened. I'm at death's door. Poor wretch that I am. Ye gods, what's to become of me? This nasty man is going to kill me. St Anthony and all the Saints, protect me. I'll shell out bags of phynance and even burn candles to you. Lord God, what's to become of me? (*He weeps and sobs.*)

MA UBU. There's only one course to adopt, Pa Ubu.

PA UBU. What's that, my love?

MA UBU. War!!

ALL. May God defend the right! Well and nobly spoken!

PA UBU. Oh yes, and I'll get knocked about all over again.

FIRST COUNSELLOR. Let us get the army to battle stations with all speed.

SECOND. And requisition the supplies.

THIRD. Mobilize the artillery, man the fortresses.

FOURTH. And set aside enough money to pay the troops.

PA UBU. Ah, not likely! I'm going to do you in, you. I'm not giving any money away. What an idea! I used to be paid to make war and now I have to do it at my own expense. No, by my green candle, let's have a war since you're all so steamed up about it, but let's not spend a single sou.

ALL. Long live war, three cheers for the war.

SCENE EIGHT

The Camp outside Warsaw.

[*On the right, a mill with a practicable window. On the left, rocks. Backdrop showing the ocean.*
Enter the POLISH ARMY, *with* GENERAL LASKI *at their head, singing a marching song:*

My uniform has buttons one, thunder a gun,
My uniform has buttons two, first of the few,
Buttons one, two, three four,
Gone to the War!
Five, six, seven, eight,
Buttons are great,
Nine, ten and eleven,
Buttons are heaven,
Twelve, thirteen, fourteen
Buttons to clean,
Fifteen, sixteen, seventeen, eighteen,
Buttons awaiting,
Nineteen, twenty,
Buttons aplenty.
My tunic has thirty buttons,
Boozers and gluttons,
Forty, fifty, sixty more,
Buttons galore,
Seventy, eighty, ninety-six
Buttons for kicks!
A hundred buttons on my chest
To shine with the rest.
My tunic has fifty thousand buttons!

GENERAL LASKI. Division, halt! Left turn, about face! Right turn, dress your ranks! Eyes front! Stand at ease. Soldiers, I am pleased with you. Never forget that you are military men

and that military men make the best soldiers. To march in the
paths of glory and victory, you should first put the whole
weight of your body on your right leg, and then step out
smartly, left leg foremost . . . Attention! File off: by the right
. . . to the right! Division, forward! eyes right, quick march!
Left right, left right . . .

The SOLDIERS, *with* LASKI *at their head, march off, shouting.*]*

SOLDIERS. Long live Poland! God save Old Ubu!

PA UBU. Come on, Ma, hand me my breastplate and my little
wooden pick. I'll soon be so cluttered up that I won't be
able to run if they chase me.

MA UBU. Pooh! What a coward!

PA UBU. Drat, there's my pschittasword slipping off, and my
phynance-hook won't stay put either! I'll never be ready,
and the Russians are advancing and will certainly kill me.

A PALCONTENT. Hey, Lord Ubu, your nearole-incisors are
falling down.

PA UBU. Urghh! Me I kill you with my pschittahook and my
face-chopper. Now you dead.

MA UBU. How handsome he looks in his breastplate and helmet, just like an armour-plated pumpkin.

PA UBU. Ah! now I shall mount my horse. Gentlemen, lead in
the phynance charger.

MA UBU. Pa Ubu, your horse will never be able to carry you,
it hasn't been fed for five days and is half dead.

PA UBU. That's a good one! They rook me a dollar a day for
that old nag and it can't even carry me. Are you making fun
of me, horn of Ubu, or are you pocketing the cash, perhaps,
eh? (MA UBU *blushes and lowers her eyes.*) All right, bring me
out another beast, but I refuse to go on foot, hornstrumpot!
(*An enormous horse is led in.*) I'm going to get up on it. Oh,
I'd better sit down, otherwise I'll fall off! (*The horse ambles
off.*) Hi, stop this runaway brute! God almighty, I shall fall
off and suddenly find I'm dead!!

MA UBU. Oh, what an idiot. Ah, he's back in his saddle again.
No, he's fallen off.

* From *Ubu sur la Butte, II,* 1.

PA UBU. Horn of physics, I'm half dead, but no matter, I'm off to the war and I'll kill everyone. Woe betide any of you who step out of line, because I'll give him the full treatment, including a session of nose and tooth twisting and tongue pulling.

MA UBU. Good luck, Ubu, my lord and master.

PA UBU. I forgot to tell you, I'm making you regent. But I'm taking the account-books with me, so if you try to cheat me you'll be in for a hot time. I'm leaving the Palcontent Gyron as your assistant. Farewell, Madam.

MA UBU. Farewell, great commander, and mind you kill the Tsar good and proper.

PA UBU. Don't you worry about that. Nose and tooth twisting, tongue pulling and perforation of the nearoles by my little wooden pick.

He clatters off, to the sound of fanfares.

MA UBU (*alone*). Now that that overstuffed dummy is out of the way, let's get down to business, assassinate Boggerlas and get our hands on the treasures of Poland.

Act Four

SCENE ONE

The crypt of the former Kings of Poland in Warsaw Cathedral.

MA UBU. Now, where can that treasure be? None of these flagstones sound hollow. Well, I've certainly counted thirteen stones from the tomb of Ladislas the Great, keeping to the wall, but there's nothing. Someone's made a fool of me. Ah! wait a minute, this flagstone sounds hollow. To work, Ma Ubu. Let's get down to it, and we'll soon have it prised up. It won't budge. Let's try inserting the end of this phynance-hook and hope that it will be working for once. Ah, there it is! There's the gold all mixed up with the bones of the kings. Into our sack with the whole lot. Oh, what's that noise? Can there still be anyone alive in these ancient vaults? No, it's nothing, let's take the lot and get out quick. These gold pieces will look far better in the light of day than buried in the graves of these old princes. Now we'll put the stone back. What's that? That noise again. This place is beginning to give me the creeps. I'll come back tomorrow for the rest of the gold.

A VOICE (*rising from the tomb of John Sigismund*). Never, Ma Ubu!

Ma Ubu escapes in a panic by way of a secret door, taking the stolen gold with her.

[*Act Four, Scene One of* Ubu Rex *may be replaced by Act Two, Scene Two, of* Ubu sur la Butte, *which commences with Ma Ubu's closing speech in* Ubu Rex, *Act Three, Scene Eight, as follows:*

MA UBU. Now that that overstuffed dummy is out of the way, let's get down to business, assassinate Boggerlas and get our hands on the treasures of Poland. First, the treasures. Hey, Gyron, come and help me.

GYRON. Help you do what, mistress?

MA UBU. Everything! My dear husband desires you to take over
from him completely while he's off at the wars. So tonight . . .

GYRON. Oh! mistress!

MA UBU. Don't blush, darling! In any case, with your com-
plexion it's invisible.* But to work, give me a hand carting
these treasures away.

Sung very fast, while carrying off the objects described in the song.

MA UBU. Can I believe my eyes or not?
I see a pot . . . a Polish pot!

GYRON. A bed-side rug of reindeer skin,
Once trod on by the poor dead queen!

MA UBU. A faithful portrait, I am sure,
Of my lord and spouse whom I adore.

GYRON. Bottles whose contents made Poles sing
In the good old days of the Drunken King.

MA UBU (*brandishing a pschittapump*).
And here's the special Turkish hookah
Made for Queen Leczinska.

GYRON. These rolls of paper in their crate
Are secret documents of state.

MA UBU (*brandishing a lavatory brush*).
And the little sceptre made of straw
Which kept the peace in old Warsaw.

MA UBU. Hey! I can hear a noise! It must be Pa Ubu coming
back. So soon?! Quick, run for it!

They run off, dropping their treasures on the way.]

SCENE TWO

The Main Square in Warsaw.

BOGGERLAS *and his men*, PEOPLE *and* SOLDIERS.

BOGGERLAS. Forward, my friends! Long live Poland and
King Wenceslas! That old scoundrel Ubu has fled, which
only leaves Old Mother Ubu and her Palcontent to deal with.
I ask only to march at your head and restore the royal
succession of my ancestors.

* Jarry specifies, in *Ubu sur la Butte*, that the Palcontent Gyron is
to be played by a Negro. (*Editor's note.*)

ALL. Long live Boggerlas!

BOGGERLAS. And we shall abolish all the taxes imposed by that horrible Old Ubu.

ALL. Hurrah! Forward! Onward to the palace! Let's wipe out the whole vile breed!

BOGGERLAS. Aha! There's the old hag coming out on to the palace steps, surrounded by her guards.

MA UBU. What can I do for you, gentlemen? Ah! It's Boggerlas.

The crowd throw stones.

FIRST GUARD. All the windows are broken.

SECOND GUARD. By St George, they've got me.

THIRD GUARD. I die, by God's holy horn!

BOGGERLAS. Keep throwing stones, my friends.

PALCONTENT GYRON. Ho! So that's the way it is!

He draws his sword and plunges into the crowd, wreaking terrible carnage.

BOGGERLAS. Defend yourself, cowardly bumpkin! I challenge you to single combat!

GYRON. I'm done for!

BOGGERLAS. Victory, my friends! Now for Ma Ubu! (*Trumpets sound.*) Ah, here come the nobles. Quick, let's seize the wicked harpy.

ALL. Yes, she'll do, until we can string up the old bandit himself.

MA UBU *escapes, pursued by all the* POLES. *Rifle shots and hails of stones.*

SCENE THREE

The POLISH ARMY *marching through the Ukraine.*

PA UBU. By God's holy horn, by God's third leg, we shall certainly perish, for we are dying of thirst and are quite exhausted. Honourable soldier, have the kindness to carry our phynancial helmet, and you, honourable lancer, take charge of our pschitt-scissors and our physick-stick to relieve our burden for, I repeat, we are fatigued.

The soldiers obey.

HEADS. Ho there, Sire! Ain't it odd that there's no sign of the Russians yet.

PA UBU. It is most regrettable that the state of our finances does not permit us to own a carriage commensurate with our dimensions, for, since we were afraid of our mount collapsing under us, we have completed the whole journey on foot, leading the animal on the rein. But as soon as we get back to Poland we shall, by making use of our knowledge of physics and in consultation with our learned advisers, invent a wind-driven carriage capable of transporting the entire army.

TAILS. Here comes Nicolas Renski at full speed.

PA UBU. What's he in such a flap about?

RENSKI. All is lost, Sire. The Poles have rebelled, Gyron has been killed, and Madam Ubu has fled to the mountains.

PA UBU. Night-bird, creature of ill omen, shiftless mongrel! Where did you snuffle up that rubbish? Here's a fine kettle of fish. Well, who's responsible, eh? Boggerlas, I'll bet. Where have you just come from?

RENSKI. Warsaw, noble Lord.

PA UBU. Pschitt upon you, young fellow, if I believed you I'd order the whole army to about turn and march back in the direction it's just come from. But, honourable infant, you are feather-brained and therefore light-headed, and have been dreaming foolish dreams. Go to the forward posts, my lad, and you'll see that the Russians aren't far away. In fact we'll soon have to strike out with all our arms, including the pschittical, phynancial and physical varieties.

GENERAL LASKI. Master Ubu, do you see? That's the Russian army down there in the plain.

PA UBU. You're right, it's the Russians! Here's a fine state of affairs. If only there was some way of escape – but no, we're on a hilltop and exposed to attack on every side.

THE ARMY. The Russians! The enemy!

PA UBU. Come, gentlemen, let us take up our battle positions.

We'll stay on top of this hill and we'll not be so silly as to venture down. I shall remain in your midst like an animated citadel, and the rest of you will gravitate around me. I recommend you to load your rifles with as many bullets as they will hold, since eight bullets can kill eight Russians and that's just so many more I won't have on my back. We shall station the light infantry around the bottom of the hill to take the brunt of the Russian attack and slay a few of them, with the cavalry behind to charge around and add to the confusion, and the artillery set up around this windmill here to fire into the general mêlée. As for ourselves, we shall assume our command position inside the windmill, fire through the window with our phynancial pistol, bar the door with our physick-stick, and if anyone tries to break in he'd better look out for our pschittahook!!!

OFFICERS. Your orders shall be carried out, Lord Ubu.

PA UBU. Ah, well that's all right, then. We shall be victorious. What time is it?

[*The sound* 'cuckoo!' *is heard three times.**]

GENERAL LASKI. Eleven o'clock in the morning.

PA UBU. Let's have lunch, then. The Russians never attack before noon. Tell the soldiers, my Lord General, to fall out for a quick piss and then strike up our anthem, the Financial Song.

LASKI *goes out.*

SOLDIERS AND PALCONTENTS. Long live Old Ubu, our great Financier! Ting, ting, ting; ting, ting, ting; ting, ting, tating!

PA UBU. Oh, the fine fellows, I adore them. (*A cannon-ball whizzes past and breaks the sail of the windmill.*) Hooh! Hah! I'm frightened. Great God, I'm dead! No, I'm all right after all.

[*Or substitute the following ending to Scene Three, from* Ubu sur la Butte, *Act Two, Scene Three:*

PA UBU. Let's have lunch, then. The Russians never attack

* Stage direction from *Ubu sur la Butte*.

before noon. Tell the soldiers, my Lord General, to fall out for a quick piss and then strike up our anthem, the Song of Poland.

GENERAL LASKI. 'Ten-shun! By the right! By the left! Form a circle! Two steps backward ... march! Dismiss!

THE ARMY *marches out, accompanied by flourishes of trumpets.* PA UBU *starts to sing, and* THE ARMY *marches back in time to join in the chorus at the end of the first verse.*

Song of Poland

PA UBU. Let's drain it dry,
  Every drop from this jug!
  Here's mud in your eye,
  As it goes down glug-glug.
CHORUS. Glug-glug, glug-glug, glug-glug.
PA UBU. When thirst grips my throat
  And makes me feel grumpy,
  I push out the boat
  And get drunk as an M.P.
CHORUS. Pee-pee, pee-pee, pee-pee.
PA UBU. By my beard in full bloom,
  I dare any mocker
  To sneer at the plume
  Of my great Lancer's chapka.
CHORUS. Ca-ca, ca-ca, ca-ca.
PA UBU. Bloated face, trembling hand
  Are the drunkard's just due:
  So hurrah for Poland
  And good old Ubu!
CHORUS. Poo-poo, poo-poo, poo-poo.

PA UBU. Oh the fine fellows, I adore them. (*A cannon-ball whizzes past and breaks the sail of the windmill.*) Hooh! Hah! I'm frightened. Great God, I'm dead! No, I'm all right after all.]

SCENE FOUR

THE SAME, A CAPTAIN, *then* THE RUSSIAN ARMY.

A CAPTAIN (*coming in*). Lord Ubu, Sire, the Russians are attacking.

PA UBU. Well, what do you expect me to do about it? I didn't
tell them to. Nevertheless, Gentlemen of the Phynances, let
us prepare ourselves for battle.

GENERAL LASKI. Another cannon-ball!

PA UBU. Oh, I've had enough of this. It's raining lead and steel
around here, and our precious person might even suffer
some damage. Let's get out of here.

*They all descend the slope at the double. The battle opens. They
disappear in clouds of smoke at the foot of the hill.*

A RUSSIAN (*striking out*). For God and the Tsar!

RENSKI. Oh, I'm done for.

PA UBU. Forward! Hey you, take that, sir, for scaring me, you
drunken clot, by waving that rusty old musket at me.

THE RUSSIAN. Try this then! (*He fires his revolver at him.*)

PA UBU. Ooh! ah! ouch! I'm hit, I'm holed, I'm perforated,
I've received extreme unction, I'm buried. Oh well, not
quite. Ah, I've got him. (*He tears him into little bits.*) There,
now start something up again!

GENERAL LASKI. Forward, one last effort, men. Once across
the trench and victory is ours.

PA UBU. Are you quite sure? So far, my brow is wreathed with
lumps rather than laurels.

RUSSIAN CAVALRY. Hurrah! Make way for the Tsar!

The TSAR *arrives, accompanied by* MACNURE *in disguise.*

A POLE. Oh, Christ! Every man for himself, here comes the
Tsar.

ANOTHER. My God, he's over the trench!

ANOTHER. Bing! Bang! There's four of our men annihilated
by that big bugger of a lieutenant.

MACNURE. What, the rest of you haven't had enough yet?
All right then, here's one for you, Jan Sobieski! (*He slays
him.*) I'll settle your hash, the lot of you!

He makes a bloodbath of Poles.

PA UBU. Forward, my friends. Get hold of that lousy sod!
Make mincemeat of the Russians! Victory is ours. Three
cheers for the Red Eagle!

ALL. Forward! Hurrah! By God's third leg, let's get that big bugger.

MACNURE. By St George, I've come a cropper.

PA UBU (*recognizing him*). Ah! so it's you, M'Nure. Well, well, well, my dear old friend! We are delighted to see you again, and so is the rest of the company. I shall roast you over a slow fire. Gentlemen of the Phynances, pray light a fire. Oh! Ah! Oh! I'm a dead man. That must have been a cannon-ball that just hit me. Dear God, I beseech you, forgive me my sins. Ouch! It was a cannon-ball, all right.

MACNURE. Ha ha! It was a cap-pistol.

PA UBU. Ah, so you're making fun of me, are you? Well, that's the last time! You've had it now. (*He throws himself on* MACNURE *and tears him to pieces.*)

GENERAL LASKI. Master Ubu, we are advancing on all fronts.

PA UBU. So I see. But I'm all in, I'm dented all over with kicks, and I think I'll sit down and take it easy. Ooh, my poor gutbag!

GENERAL LASKI. Go and puncture the Tsar's gutbag, Pa Ubu.

PA UBU. Ha yes, that's the ticket. Let's get at him. Now then, pschittasword, to your duty; and you, phynance-hook, don't lag behind. Physick-stick, go to work in eager emulation of them and share with the little wooden pick the honour of slaughtering, scooping out and stuffing the Muscovite Emperor. Forward, my noble phynance charger. (*He hurls himself upon the* TSAR.)

A RUSSIAN OFFICER. Look out, Your Majesty!

PA UBU. Take that, you! Oo! Ow! I say, do you mind! I mean, please excuse me, Sir, leave me alone. Ouch! I didn't do it on purpose. (*He runs away, pursued by* THE TSAR.) Holy Virgin, this lunatic's chasing me! Dear God, what did I do? Oh, goodness, there's still the trench to get across: I can feel his breath down my neck and the trench is looming up in front of me! Courage – eyes shut!

He jumps the trench. THE TSAR *falls in.*

THE TSAR. Now I'm in the soup!

THE POLES. Hurrah! The Tsar's fallen in!

PA UBU. Oof! I hardly dare look back! Ha, he's stuck in the trench, and they're bopping him on the top. That's it, gallant Poles, bash him hard, there's room for plenty of whacks on his surface, the wretch. I don't dare look at him, myself! And yet it's all turned out as we foretold, the physick-stick has worked miracles and there's no doubt that we would certainly have made mincemeat of him if an inexplicable terror had not suddenly arisen within us to combat and annihilate the mechanism of our bravery. But we were obliged suddenly to turn tail, and we owe our safety entirely to our skill in horsemanship and to the solid hocks of our phynance charger who is as swift as he is strong and whose agility is proverbial, and likewise to the depth of the trench which happened to lie so opportunely beneath the feet of the enemy of ourselves the aforementioned and here-present Master of Phynances. Hmm! what a pretty speech, a pity no one was listening. Right, back to business!

The RUSSIAN DRAGOONS *charge and rescue the* TSAR.

GENERAL LASKI. It looks like they're routing us.

PA UBU. Aha! Then I'd better get out while the going's good. Now then, my brave Poles, forward! I mean, backward!

THE POLES. Every man for himself!

PA UBU. Come on, let's go! What a mob, what a rout, what a stampede! How shall I ever get out of this mess? (*He is jostled.*) Hey, you there, mind where you're going, or you will certainly sample the fiery valour of the Master of Phynances. Ah, he's gone. Now let's beat a hasty retreat while Laski isn't watching.

(*He runs off.* THE TSAR *and* THE RUSSIAN ARMY *cross the stage in pursuit of* THE POLES.)

SCENE FIVE

A cave in Lithuania. It is snowing.

PA UBU, *the* PALCONTENTS, HEADS *and* TAILS.

PA UBU. What vile weather! It's freezing hard enough to split a rock, and the person of the Master of Phynances finds itself excessively inconvenienced thereby.

HEADS. Hoy there! Mister Ubu, Sir, have you recovered from your terror and your running away?

PA UBU. Yes, I'm not frightened any more, but my guts are still running.

TAILS. Pooh! What a crappy creature!

PA UBU. You there, Mister Tails, how's your nearole?

TAILS. As well as can be expected, Sire, considering the fact that it is not well at all. In consequench of whish, the lead inside it makes it tilt earthwards since I haven't been able to extract the bullet.

PA UBU. How splendid! You're like me, boy, always spoiling for a fight. As for me, I displayed the greatest valour, and without endangering myself in the least I massacred four of the enemy with my bare hands, not counting all those who were already dead when I dispatched them.

TAILS. Hey, Heads, do you have any idea what happened to little Renski?

HEADS. He got a bullet through the head.

PA UBU. Just as the poppy and the dandelion are scythed down in the flower of their youth by the pitiless scythe of the pitiless scyther who pitilessly scythes their pitiful pans, so poor Renski has played the pretty poppy's pitiful part – he fought gallantly, but there were just too many Russians around.

HEADS and TAILS (together). Hoy there! Mister!

AN ECHO. Hhrumph!

HEADS. What's that noise? On guard with our pea-shooters and catapults.

PA UBU. Oh, no, damn it, not the Russians again! I've had enough of them! Any more nonsense from them and I'll fuggem up good and proper.

SCENE SIX

THE SAME. *Enter* A BEAR.

TAILS. Hoy there, Mister Phynance!

PA UBU. Oh, my! Look at that little bow-wow. Isn't it cute?

HEADS. Look out! Oh, what an enormous bear. Where's my ammunition?

PA UBU. A bear! Arghh! what a monstrous beast. Oh, poor little me, I'm a gonner. God save me! And it's coming for me. No, it's got hold of Tails. Whew! that was a close shave.

The BEAR *throws itself on* TAILS. HEADS *attacks it with a knife.* UBU *takes refuge on a rock.*

TAILS. Help, Heads! Help! Come to my aid, Mister Ubu, Sir!

PA UBU. Nothing doing! Look after yourself, my friend. Just at the moment we are reciting our Pater Noster. Everyone will have his turn to get eaten.

HEADS. I've got it. I've got a half-nelson on it.

TAILS. Keep it up, pal, it's beginning to let go of me.

PA UBU. *Sanctificetur nomen tuum.*

TAILS. Cowardly sod!

HEADS. Ow! it's biting me! Oh, Lord save us, I'm as good as dead.

PA UBU. *Fiat voluntas tua!*

TAILS. Ah! I've managed to wound the brute.

HEADS. Hurrah! it's bleeding.

While the PALCONTENTS *yell and shout, the* BEAR *bellows in pain and* UBU *continues to mumble.*

TAILS. Hold it tight while I go get my explosive knuckle-duster.

PA UBU. *Panem nostrum quotidianum da nobis hodie.*

HEADS. Hurry up, I can't hold out much longer.

PA UBU. *Sicut et nos dimittimus debitoribus nostris.*

TAILS. Ah, here it is.

A tremendous explosion. The BEAR *drops dead.*

HEADS *and* TAILS. Victory.

PA UBU. *Sed libera nos a malo.* Amen. Well, is he really dead? Can I come down off my rock?

HEADS (*contemptuously*). Do whatever you like.

PA UBU (*climbing down*). You may pride yourselves that if you be still alive and still trampling underfoot the snows of Lithuania, you owe the fact entirely to the generous virtue of the Master of Phynances, who has strained his integument, acquired a slipped disc and ruptured his larynx in reciting paternosters for your salvation, and who has wielded the spiritual weapon of prayer with a courage equal to the dexterity you have shown in wielding the temporal weapon of the here-present Palcontent Tails' explosive knuckle-duster. We carried our own devotion even further, in that we did not hesitate to climb to the top of a very high rock so that our prayers should have less far to travel to mount to heaven.

HEADS. Lousy swine!

PA UBU. My, what a fat animal. Thanks to me, you've got something to eat. What a belly, gentlemen! The Greeks would have found it more comfortable in there than in their wooden horse, and we were very near, dear friends, to being able to verify with our own eyes its interior capacity.

HEADS. I'm dying of hunger. What's there to eat?

TAILS. The bear!

PA UBU. My poor friends, are you going to eat it raw? We don't have anything to start a fire with.

HEADS. We've got our gun-flints, haven't we?

PA UBU. Ah yes, that's true. And besides, I think I can see just over there a small copse where we should be able to find some dry branches. Go and fetch some, Mister Tails, Sire.

TAILS *trudges off across the snow.*

HEADS. And now, Mister Ubu, Sire, go ahead and carve up the bear.

PA UBU. Oh, no! The creature may not be quite dead yet. In any case, since you're already half eaten yourself and bitten all over, you're just the man for that job. I shall light a fire while waiting for the other knave to bring the wood.

HEADS *starts carving up the* BEAR.

PA UBU. Oo, look out! I distinctly saw it move.

HEADS. But, Mister Ubu, Sire, it's already cold.

PA UBU. Oh, that's a pity, it would have been nicer to eat it while still warm. This is bound to give the Master of Phynances an attack of indigestion.

HEADS (*aside*). He really is repulsive. (*Aloud.*) Give us a hand, Mister Ubu, I can't do the whole job myself.

PA UBU. No, I have no intention of lifting a finger. I happen to be very tired.

TAILS (*coming back*). What snow, my friends, anyone would think we were in cold Castille or the North Pole. Night is beginning to fall. In an hour it will be dark. Let's hurry up while there's still some light.

PA UBU. Yes, do you hear that, Heads? Hurry up. Hurry up, both of you! Put the beast on a spit and roast it quick. I'm hungry, you know.

HEADS. Ah! that's the last straw! You either share the work or you get nothing to eat; understand, you fat pig?

PA UBU. Oh well, it's all the same to me. I'd just as soon eat it raw, as a matter of fact; it's your stomachs that will suffer. In any case, I'm sleepy.

TAILS. He's hopeless, Heads! Let's get dinner ready by ourselves. He won't have any, that's all. If we feel generous we might throw him a few bones.

HEADS. Agreed. Ah, the fire's catching!

PA UBU. Oh, that's nice, it's getting warm now. But I see Russians everywhere. God Almighty, what a rout! Aah!

He falls asleep.

TAILS. I wonder if Renski was telling the truth when he said that Ma Ubu really was dethroned. It wouldn't surprise me at all.

HEADS. Let's finish cooking the meal.

TAILS. No, we have more important things to do. I think we should find out whether these rumours are true or not.

HEADS. You're right. Should we desert Pa Ubu or stay with him?

TAILS. Let's sleep on it. We can decide what to do tomorrow morning.

HEADS. No, let's slip away now, under cover of darkness.

TAILS. Let's go, then.

They leave.

SCENE SEVEN

PA UBU (*talking in his sleep*). Hey, mister Russian dragoon, Sir, don't shoot in this direction, there's someone here. Ah! there's M'Nure, he's got a nasty look about him, just like a bear. And there's Boggerlas coming after me! The bear, the bear! Ah, it's down! What a tough monster, great God! No, I won't lend a hand. Go away, Boggerlas! Do you hear me, you lout? Here's Renski now, and the Tsar! Oh! they're going to hit me. Ugh, there's madam my female! Where did you get all that gold? You've stolen my gold, you slut, you've been scrabbling around in my tomb which is in Warsaw Cathedral, not far from the Moon. I've been dead a long time, yes, it's Boggerlas who killed me and I'm buried at Warsaw by the side of Ladislas the Great, and also at Cracow by the side of Jan Sigismund, and also at Thorn in the casemate with M'Nure! There it is again. Be off with you, accursed bear. You look just like M'Nure. And you smell just like M'Nure. Do you hear me, beast of Satan? No, he can't hear me, the Phynance-extortioners have perforated his nearoles. Debraining, killing off, perforation of nearoles, money grabbing and drinking oneself to death, that's the life for a Phynance-extortioner, and the Master of Phynances revels in such joys.

He falls silent and sleeps.

Act Five

SCENE ONE

It is night. PA UBU *is asleep.* MA UBU *enters without seeing him.*
It is pitch dark.

MA UBU. Shelter at last! I'm alone here, which is fine as far as
I'm concerned, but what a dreadful journey: crossing the
whole of Poland in four days! Every possible misfortune
struck me at the same moment. As soon as that great, fat oaf
had clattered off on his nag I crept into the crypt to grab the
treasure, but then everything went wrong. I just escaped
being stoned to death by Boggerlas and his madmen. I lost
my gallant Palcontent Gyron who was so enamoured of my
charms that he swooned with delight every time he saw me
and even, I've been told, every time he didn't see me – and
there can be no higher love than that. Poor boy, he would
have let himself be cut in half for my sake, and the proof is
that Boggerlas cut him in quarters. Biff, bam, boom! Ooh, I
thought it was all up with me. Then I fled for my life with
the bloodthirsty mob hard on my heels. I managed to get
out of the palace and reach the Vistula, but all the bridges
were guarded. I swam across the river, hoping to shake off
my pursuers. The entire nobility rallied and joined in the
chase. I nearly breathed my last a thousand times, half
smothered by the surrounding Poles all screaming for my
blood. Finally, I escaped their clutches, and after four days
of trudging through the snows of what was once my kingdom
have at last reached refuge here. I've had nothing to eat or
drink these past four days, and Boggerlas breathing down
my neck the whole time. Now here I am, safe at last. Ah!
I'm dead with exhaustion and hunger. But I'd give a lot to
know what became of my big fat buffoon, I mean to say my
esteemed spouse. Lord, how I've skinned him, and relieved

him of his rix-dollars! I've certainly rolled him plenty! And his phynance charger that was dying of hunger – it didn't get oats to munch very often, poor beast! It was fun while it lasted, but alas, I had to leave my treasure behind in Warsaw, where it's up for grabs.

PA UBU (*beginning to wake up*). Catch Ma Ubu, chop off her nears!

MA UBU. My God, where am I? I'm losing my mind. But, no, heavens above, for –

> Thanks be to God, by my side I behold
> The sleeping form of Sir Ubu the Bold.

Let's play it cool. Well, you fat oaf, have you slept well?

PA UBU. No, very badly! Oof, that bear was tough! Battle to the death between the voracious and the coriaceous, but the voracious completely ate up and devoured the coriaceous, as you will see when it gets light. Do you hear me, brave Palcontents?

MA UBU. What's he babbling about? He's even stupider than when he left. Who's he having a go at?

PA UBU. Tails, Heads, answer me, pschittbag! Where are you? Oh, I'm scared. But somebody spoke, who was it? Not the bear, I hope. Pschitt! Where are my matches? I must have lost them during the battle.

MA UBU. Let's take advantage of the situation and the darkness. Let's pretend to be a supernatural apparition and make him promise to forgive our peculations.

PA UBU. But by St Anthony, someone's speaking! By God's third leg, I'll be hanged if someone isn't speaking.

MA UBU (*in a great hollow voice*). Yes, Mister Ubu, someone is indeed speaking, and with the tongue of the archangel's trumpet that shall summon the dead from their graves to meet their judgement! Listen to that terrible voice. It is the voice of the archangel Gabriel who is incapable of giving anything but good advice.

PA UBU. He can stuff his advice.

MA UBU. Don't interrupt or I shall fall silent and you'll find your bumboozle's on the hot seat!

PA UBU. Ah! by my strumpot! I'll keep quiet, I won't breathe
a word. Pray continue, Mrs Apparition.

MA UBU. We were saying, Mister Ubu, that you were a fat oaf.

PA UBU. Hmm! Fat, yes, I grant you that.

MA UBU. Shut up, goddammit!

PA UBU. Hey! Angels aren't supposed to swear!

MA UBU (*aside*). Pschitt! (*Continuing.*) You are married, Mister
Ubu?

PA UBU. Too true. To a vile hag.

MA UBU. You mean, to a charming lady.

PA UBU. An old horror. She sprouts claws all over, it's impossible to get one's hand up her anywhere.

MA UBU. You should give her a hand up kindly and gently,
honest Mister Ubu, and were you to do so you would see
that she was just as appealing as Aphrodite.

PA UBU. Who did you say wears an appalling frayed nightie?

MA UBU. You are not listening, Mister Ubu. Lend us a more
attentive ear. (*Aside.*) But we must hurry, for dawn is breaking. Mister Ubu, your wife is a delightful and adorable
person, who hasn't a single defect.

PA UBU. On the contrary, she's got the lot.

MA UBU. Silence, Sir! Your wife has never been unfaithful to
you!

PA UBU. Only because the old hag's so ugly that no man in his
right mind would ever give her a chance of being unfaithful!

MA UBU. She doesn't drink!

PA UBU. Not since I kept the cellar door locked. Before that,
she was plastered by seven in the morning and perfumed
with the scent of brandy. Now that she can afford to perfume
herself with heliotrope she doesn't smell any worse. One
stink's as good as another, as far as I'm concerned. But now
I have to get plastered all on my own.

MA UBU. Silly idiot! Your wife doesn't steal your bags of gold.

PA UBU. Come off it!

MA UBU. She doesn't pocket a single penny!

PA UBU. As witness our noble and unfortunate phynance
charger who, having been starved for three months, had to
go through the entire campaign being led by the reins across

the Ukraine, until the poor beast finally died in harness.

MA UBU. All this is false. Your wife is an absolute saint, and you are a great monster.

PA UBU. All this is true. My wife's a lazy slut and you're a great booby!

MA UBU. Have a care, Mister Ubu.

PA UBU. You're right – I was forgetting to whom I was speaking. I take it all back.

MA UBU. You killed King Wenceslas.

PA UBU. That wasn't *my* fault, oh no, it was Ma Ubu who egged me on.

MA UBU. You had Boleslas and Ladislas assassinated.

PA UBU. Serve them right! They tried to hit me!

MA UBU. You not only broke your promise to M'Nure, you killed him as well.

PA UBU. I'd rather it was me than him that reigned in Lithuania. For the moment it's neither of us. At least you can see it's not me.

MA UBU. There's only one way for you to gain redemption of your sins.

PA UBU. What's that? I wouldn't at all mind becoming a holy man, in fact I'd like to be a bishop and see my name in the calendar.

MA UBU. You must forgive Madam Ubu for having pocketed a little bit of your spare cash.

PA UBU. All right, I'll tell you what! I'll forgive her when she's handed over all the loot, when she's been soundly walloped, and when she's brought my phynance charger back to life.

MA UBU. He's got that damn horse on the brain. Oh, it's beginning to get light. I'm lost!

PA UBU. Still, I'm glad to learn definitely that my dear wife has been swindling me. I have it now on the best authority. *Omnis a Deo scientia*, which means: *Omnis*, all; *a Deo*, wisdom; *scientia*, comes from God. Which explains the whole miraculous revelation. But Madam Apparition has fallen silent. What healing draught can I offer her to bring back her voice? For her conversation was most amusing. Why, it's daybreak already. Ha, by heavens and by my phynance charger, it's Ma Ubu!

MA UBU (*brazening it out*). That's not true. I shall excommunicate you.

PA UBU. Carrion!

MA UBU. Oh, what blasphemy.

PA UBU. This is too much. I can see perfectly well that it's you, you silly old bag. What the devil are you doing here?

MA UBU. Gyron is dead and the Poles were after me, so I thought I'd better get out while the going was good.

PA UBU. The Russians were after *me*, so *I* thought I'd better get out while the going was good. Ah well, they say that great minds think alike.

MA UBU. They can say that if they want, but my great mind thinks it's just met a pea-brained idiot.

PA UBU. Oh, very well, and in a moment it's going to meet a palmiped.

He hurls the bear at her.

MA UBU (*falling prostrate under the weight of the bear*). Great God! How horrible! I'm dying! I'm suffocating! It's biting me! It's swallowing me! It's digesting me!

PA UBU. It's dead, you freak! Oh, but maybe it isn't after all. Lord, no, it's not dead, let's escape. (*Climbing up onto his rock again.*) *Pater noster qui es . . .*

MA UBU (*emerging from beneath the bear*). Now where's he got to?

PA UBU. Oh Lord, there she is again! Am I going to be saddled with this stupid bitch for ever? Is that bear dead?

MA UBU. Saddle yourself, you donkey. Yes, it's stiff already. How did it get here?

PA UBU (*confused*). I don't know. Oh yes, I remember. It wanted to eat Heads and Tails and I killed it single-handed with one blow of my paternoster.

MA UBU. Heads, Tails, paternoster – what's he going on about? He's off his rocker, the silly chump.

PA UBU. It's the gospel truth, I'm telling you, you bumboozle-faced idiot.

MA UBU. Tell me all about your campaign, Captain Ubu.

PA UBU. No, no, it would take too long. All I know is that despite my incontestable valour, everyone defeated me.

MA UBU. What, even the Poles?

PA UBU. They were all shouting 'Long live Wenceslas and Boggerlas!' I thought they were going to tear me to pieces. What madmen! And then they lynched Renski.

MA UBU. I couldn't care less! You know that Boggerlas slaughtered the Palcontent Gyron?

PA UBU. I couldn't care less! And then they lynched poor Laski.

MA UBU. I couldn't care less!

PA UBU. Oh, that's quite enough from you. Come here, carrion, and kneel before your master. (*He seizes her and forces her to her knees.*) You are about to undergo the extreme penalty.

MA UBU. Ow, ow, ow, Mister Ubu!

PA UBU. Have you quite finished with your ow, ow, ows? Because now *I'm* going to begin: twisting of the nose, tearing out of the hair, penetration of the nearoles by the little wooden pick, extraction of the brain-matter by way of the heels, laceration of the posterior, partial or even total suppression of the spinal marrow (thus confirming the fact that the victim is a spineless creature), not to mention the puncturing of the swimming-bladder, and finally the grand new version of the decollation of St John the Baptist as specified in the most Holy Scriptures of both the Old and New Testaments, as edited, corrected and perfectioned by yours truly the here-present Master of Phynances! How does that suit you, puddinghead?

He starts tearing her to pieces.

MA UBU. Mercy, mercy, Mister Ubu, Sir!

Loud noise at the entrance to the cave.

SCENE TWO

THE SAME; BOGGERLAS, *storming the cave with his* SOLDIERS.

BOGGERLAS. Forward, my friends! Long live Poland!

PA UBU. Hey there, just a minute, Mister Polack. Wait till I'm through with madam my worse half.

BOGGERLAS (*striking him*). Take that, coward, scavenger, scoundrel, infidel, Mussulman!

PA UBU (*countering*). Take that, great clot, pisspot, son of a harlot, nose-snot, bigot, faggot, gut-rot, squawking parrot, Huguenot!

MA UBU (*hitting him too*). Take that, pork-snout, layabout, whore's tout, pox-riddled spout, idle lout, boy scout, Polish Kraut.

The SOLDIERS *hurl themselves on the* UBUS *who defend themselves as best they can.*

PA UBU. Ye gods, we're getting a drubbing!

MA UBU. Let's tread on the Polacks' toes.

PA UBU. By my green candle, this is going on too long. There's another of them! Oh, if only I had my phynance charger with me here!

BOGGERLAS. Hit them, go on hitting them!

VOICES (*offstage*). Long live Pa Ubu, our great Phynancier!

PA UBU. Ah, here they are! Hurrah! Here come the Ubuists. Come on, quick march, to the rescue, phynancial gentlemen!

The PALCONTENTS *enter and throw themselves into the fight.*

TAILS. Get out, you Poles!

HEADS. Hoy, Mister Phynance, we meet once again! Come on, men, fight your way through to the entrance, and once we're outside let's run for it.

PA UBU. Oh yes, I'm very good at that. Look how Heads is hitting out around him.

BOGGERLAS. God, I'm wounded.

STANISLAS LECZINSKI. It's nothing, Sire.

BOGGERLAS. Yes, I'm all right. I just came over all peculiar
   suddenly.

JAN SOBIESKI. Hit them, go on hitting them, the scoundrels
   are getting away.

TAILS. We're almost there, follow me everybody. By consequench of whish I see daylight.

HEADS. Courage, Lord Ubu!

PA UBU. Ooh, I've just crapped in my pants. Forward, hornstrumpot! Killemoff, bleedemoff, skinnemoff, shaggemoff,
   by Ubu's horn. Ah, they're falling back.

TAILS. There's only two left guarding the door.

PA UBU (*swinging the* BEAR *round his head, and knocking them
   down with it*). That's for you! And for you! Ha, I'm outside!
   Let's get the hell out of here! Come on, the rest of you,
   follow me, and look sharp about it!

SCENE THREE

*The scene represents the Province of Livonia covered with snow.
The* UBUS *and their followers in flight.*

PA UBU. At last, I think they've abandoned the chase.

MA UBU. Yes, Boggerlas has gone off to get himself crowned.

PA UBU. He knows what he can do with his crown!

MA UBU. Oh how right you are, Old Ubu.

They vanish into the distance.

SCENE FOUR

*The bridge of a ship sailing close to the wind on the Baltic. On
the bridge,* PA UBU *and his whole* GANG.

THE CAPTAIN. What a lovely breeze!

PA UBU. It's a fact that we are moving at an almost miraculous
   speed, which I estimate at, give or take a bit, about a million
   knots an hour, and the remarkable thing about these knots
   is that once they've been tied they can't come untied again.
   And of course we have the wind in the poop.

HEADS. He's a nincompoop full of wind.

A squall comes up, the ship heels over, the sea foams.

PA UBU. Oh my God, we're capsizing. Hey, it's going all whichways, your boat, it's going to fall over.

THE CAPTAIN. All hands to leeward. Close-haul the mizzen!

PA UBU. Ah, no! What an idea! Don't all stand on the same side, it's dangerous. Just supposing the wind changed suddenly! We'd all go to the bottom and the fishes would eat us up.

THE CAPTAIN. Don't bear away. Hug the wind full and by!

PA UBU. Yes, yes, tear away. I'm in a tearing hurry, do you hear! It's your fault, you fool of a skipper, if we don't get there. We should have arrived by now. There's only one solution: I'll take over command myself. Ready about. 'Bout ship. Let go the anchor. Go about in stays, wear ship, hoist more sail, haul down sail, put the tiller hard over, up with the helm, down with the helm, full speed astern, give her more lee, splice the top gallant. How am I doing? Tight as a rivet! Meet the wave crosswise and everything will be shipshape. Avast there.

All are convulsed with laughter, the wind freshens.

THE CAPTAIN. Haul down the main jib, take a reef in the topsails.

PA UBU. That's a good one. That's not bad at all. Did you get that, Mister Crew? Boil down the main rib; roast beef and oxtails!

Several die of laughter. A wave breaks over everyone.

PA UBU. Oh, what a ducking! That is the logical result of the manoeuvres we have just ordered.

MA UBU *and* HEADS. Isn't navigation wonderful?

A second wave breaks over them.

HEADS (*drenched*). Beware of Satan and all pomps and vanities.

PA UBU. That's right, beware of sitting under pumps, it's insanitary. Hey, steward, sirrah, bring us something to drink.

They all sit down to drink.

MA UBU. Oh what bliss it will be to see our sweet France once more, and all our old friends, and our Castle of Mondragon.

PA UBU. Yes, we'll soon be there. See, we are tacking past the Castle of Elsinore at this very moment.

HEADS. The prospect of seeing my beloved Spain again has put new heart into me.

TAILS. Yes, and we'll amaze our countrymen with tales of our marvellous adventures.

PA UBU. Oh yes, there's no doubt about that. As for me, I'll be off to Paris to get myself appointed Master of Phynances.

MA UBU. That's nice. Oo, what a bump that was.

TAILS. It's nothing. We've just doubled Cape Elsinore.

HEADS. And now our gallant bark speeds like a bird over the wine-dark waves of the North Sea.

PA UBU. Wild and inhospitable ocean which laps the shores of the land called Germany, so named because it's exactly half way to Jermyn Street as the blow flies.

MA UBU. Now that's what I call erudition. It's a beautiful country, I'm told.

PA UBU. Beautiful though it may be, it's not a patch on Poland. Ah gentlemen, there'll always be a Poland. Otherwise there wouldn't be any Poles!

Ubu Cuckolded

(Ubu Cocu)

Restored in its entirety
as it was performed by
the marionettes of the
Théâtre des Phynances

Five Acts

Translated by Cyril Connolly

CHARACTERS

PA UBU	THE THREE PALCONTENTS
HIS CONSCIENCE	THE COBBLER SCYTOTO-
MA UBU	MILLE
ACHRAS	THE CROCODILE
REBONTIER	A FLUNKEY
MEMNON	A WOOLIDOG

The action takes place in the house of Achras. A door at each side of the stage. At the back, another door opening on to a 'closet'.

In five acts.

This version of *Ubu Cocu* was adapted for radio by Martin Esslin and first broadcast on the BBC Third Programme on 21st December 1965 with the following cast:

NARRATOR		Preston Lockwood
ACHRAS		Noel Howlett
PA UBU		John Sharp
HIS CONSCIENCE		John Moffatt
CRAPENTAKE		Peter Pratt
BINANJITTERS	} Palcontents	Brian Hewlett
FOURZEARS		Gordon Faith
MA UBU		Margaret Wolfit
REBONTIER		Ralph Truman
SCYTOTOMILLE		Ronald Baddiley
MEMNON		Geoffrey Matthews

Produced by Martin Esslin. Music by John Beckett.

Act One

ACHRAS. Oh, but it's like this, look you, I've no grounds to be dissatisfied with my polyhedra; they breed every six weeks, they're worse than rabbits. And it's also quite true to say that the regular polyhedra are the most faithful and most devoted to their master, except that this morning the Icosahedron was a little fractious, so that I was compelled, look you, to give it a smack on each of its twenty faces. And that's the kind of language they understand. And my thesis, look you, on the habits of polyhedra – it's getting along nicely, thank you, only another twenty-five volumes!

SCENE TWO

ACHRAS, *a* FLUNKEY.

FLUNKEY. Sir, there's a bloke out here as wants a word with you. He's pulled the bell out with his ringing, and he's broken three chairs trying to sit down. (*He gives* ACHRAS *a card.*)

ACHRAS. What's all this? Herr Ubu, sometime King of Poland and Aragon, professor of pataphysics. That makes no sense at all. What's all that about? Pataphysics! Well, never mind, he sounds like a person of distinction. I should like to make a gesture of goodwill to this visitor by showing him my polyhedra. Have the gentleman come up.

SCENE THREE

ACHRAS, UBU *in a travelling costume, carrying a suitcase.*

PA UBU. Hornstrumpot, Sir! What a miserable kind of

hang-out you've got here: we've been obliged to tinkle away for more than an hour, and when your flunkeys at last make up their minds to let us in, we are confronted by such a miserable orifice that we are at a loss to understand how our strumpot managed to negotiate it.

ACHRAS. Oh but it's like this, excuse me. I was very far from expecting the visit of such a considerable personage ... otherwise, you can be sure I would have had the door enlarged. But you must forgive the humble circumstances of an old collector, who is at the same time, I venture to say, a famous scientist.

PA UBU. Say that by all means if it gives you any pleasure, but remember that you are addressing a celebrated pataphysician.

ACHRAS. Excuse me, Sir, what did you say?

PA UBU. Pataphysician. Pataphysics is a branch of science which we have invented and for which a crying need is generally experienced.

ACHRAS. Oh but it's like this, if you're a famous inventor, we'll understand each other, look you, for between great men ...

PA UBU. A little more modesty, Sir! Besides, I see no great man here except myself. But, since you insist, I have condescended to do you a most signal honour. Let it be known to you, Sir, that your establishment suits us and that we have decided to make ourselves at home here.

ACHRAS. Oh but it's like this, look you ...

PA UBU. We will dispense with your expressions of gratitude. And, by the way, I nearly forgot. Since it is hardly proper that a father should be separated from his children, we shall be joined by our family in the immediate future – Madam Ubu, together with our dear sons and daughters Ubu. They are all very quiet, decent, well-brought-up folk.

ACHRAS. Oh but it's like this, look you. I'm afraid ...

PA UBU. We quite understand. You're afraid of boring us. All right then, we'll no longer tolerate your presence here except by our kind permission. One thing more, while we are inspecting the kitchens and the dining room, you will go and look for three packing cases which we have had deposited in the hall.

ACHRAS. Oh but it's like this – fancy even thinking of moving in like that on people. It's a manifest imposture.

PA UBU. A magnificent posture! Exactly, Sir, for once in your life you've spoken the truth.

Exit ACHRAS.

SCENE FOUR

PA UBU, *then later, his* CONSCIENCE.

PA UBU. Have we any right to behave like this? Hornstrumpot, by our green candle, let us consult our Conscience. There he is, in this suitcase, all covered with cobwebs. As you can see, we don't overwork him. (*He opens the suitcase. His* CONSCIENCE *emerges in the guise of a tall, thin fellow in a shirt.*)

CONSCIENCE. Sir, and so on and so forth, be so good as to take a few notes.

PA UBU. Excuse me, Sir, we are not very partial to writing, though we have no doubt that anything you say would be most interesting. And while we're on the subject, we should like to know how you have the insolence to appear before us in your shirt tails?

CONSCIENCE. Sir, and so on and so forth, Conscience, like Truth, usually goes without a shirt. If I have put one on, it is as a mark of respect to the distinguished audience.

PA UBU. As for that, Mister or Mrs Conscience, you're making a fuss about nothing. Answer this question instead: would it be a good thing to kill Mister Achras who has had the audacity to come and insult me in my own house?

CONSCIENCE. Sir, and so on and so forth, to return good with evil is unworthy of a civilized man. Mister Achras has lodged you; Mister Achras has received you with open arms and made you free of his collection of polyhedra; Mister Achras, and so forth, is a very fine fellow and perfectly harmless; it would be a most cowardly act, and so forth, to kill a poor old man who is incapable of defending himself.

PA UBU. Hornstrumpot! Mister Conscience, are you so sure that he can't defend himself?

CONSCIENCE. Absolutely, Sir, so it would be a coward's trick to do away with him.

PA UBU. Thank you, Sir, we shan't require you further. Since there's no risk attached, we shall assassinate Mister Achras, and we shall also make a point of consulting you more frequently for you know how to give us better advice than we had anticipated. Now, into the suitcase with you! (*He closes it again.*)

CONSCIENCE. In which case, Sir, I think we shall have to leave it at that, and so on and so forth, for today.

SCENE FIVE

PA UBU, ACHRAS, *the* FLUNKEY.

Enter ACHRAS, *backwards, prostrating himself with terror before the three red packing cases pushed by the* FLUNKEY.

PA UBU (*to the* FLUNKEY). Off with you, sloven. And you, Sir, I want a word with you. I wish you every kind of prosperity and I entreat you, out of the kindness of your heart, to perform a friendly service for me.

ACHRAS. Anything, look you, which you can reasonably demand from an old professor who has given up sixty years of his life, look you, to studying the habits of polyhedra.

PA UBU. Sir, we have learned that our virtuous wife, Madam Ubu, is most abominably deceiving us with an Egyptian, by the name of Memnon, who combines the functions of a clock at dawn with driving of a sewage truck at night, and in the daytime presents himself as cornutator of our person. Hornstrumpot! We have decided to wreak the most terrible vengeance.

ACHRAS. As far as that goes, look you, Sir, as to being a cuckold I can sympathize with you.

PA UBU. We have resolved, then, to inflict a severe punishment. And we can think of nothing more appropriate to chastise the guilty, in this case, than ordeal by Impalement.

ACHRAS. Excuse me, I still don't see very clearly, look you, how I can be of any help.

PA UBU. By our green candle, Sir, since we have no wish for the execution of our sentence to be bungled, we should esteem it as a compliment if a person of your standing were to make a preliminary trial of the Stake, just to make sure that it is functioning with maximum efficiency.

ACHRAS. Oh but it's like this, look you, not on your life. That's too much. I regret, look you, that I can't perform this little service for you, but it's quite out of the question. You've stolen my house from me, look you, you've told me to bugger off, and now you want to put me to death, oh no, that's going too far.

PA UBU. Don't distress yourself, my good friend. It was only our little joke. We shall return when you have quite recovered your composure.

Exit PA UBU.

SCENE SIX

ACHRAS, *then the three* PALCONTENTS *climbing out of their packing cases.*

THE PALCONTENTS. We are the Palcontents,
 We are the Palcontents,
 With a face like a rabbit –
 Which seldom prevents
 Our bloody good habit
 Of croaking the bloke
 Wot lives on his rents.
 We are the Pals,
 We are the Cons,
 We are the Palcontents.

CRAPENTAKE. Each in his box of stainless steel
 Imprisoned all the week we kneel,
 For Sunday is the only day
 That we're allowed a getaway.
 Ears to the wind, without surprise,

We march along with vigorous step
And all the onlookers cry 'Yep,
They must be soldiers, damn their eyes!'
ALL THREE. We are the Palcontents, *etc.*
BINANJITTERS. Every morning we are called
By the Master's boot on our behind,
And, half awake, our backs are galled
By the money-satchels we have to mind.
All day the hammer never ceases
As we chip your skulls in a thousand pieces,
Until we bring to Pa Ubé
The dough from the stiffs we've croaked this day.
ALL THREE. We are the Palcontents, *etc.*

They perform a dance. ACHRAS, *terrified, sits down on a chair.*

FOURZEARS. In our ridiculous looniforms
We wander through the streets so pansy,
Or else we plug the bockle-and-jug
Of every slag who takes our fancy.
We get our eats through platinum teats,
We pee through a tap without a handle,
And we inhale the atmostale
Through a tube as bent as a Dutchman's candle!
ALL THREE. We are the Palcontents, *etc.*

They dance round ACHRAS.

ACHRAS. Oh but it's like this, look you, it's ridiculous, it
doesn't make sense at all. (*The stake rises under his chair.*) Oh
dear, I don't understand it. If you were only my polyhedra,
look you. . . . Have mercy on a poor old professor. . . . Look
. . . look you. It's out of the question! (*He is impaled and
raised in the air despite his cries. It grows pitch dark.*)
THE PALCONTENTS (*ransacking the furniture and pulling out
bags stuffed full of phynance*): Give the cash – to Pa Ubu.
Give all the cash – to Pa Ubu. Let nothing remain – not even
a sou – to go down the drain – for the Revenue. Give all the
cash – to Pa Ubu! (*Re-entering their packing-cases.*)
We are the Palcontents, *etc.*

ACHRAS *loses consciousness.*

SCENE SEVEN

ACHRAS (*impaled*), PA UBU, MA UBU.

PA UBU. By my green candle, sweet child, how happy shall we be in this house!

MA UBU. There is only one thing lacking to my happiness, my dear friend, an opportunity to greet the worthy host who has placed such entertainment at our disposal.

PA UBU. Don't let that bother you, my dear: to anticipate your wish I have had him installed in the place of honour.

He points to the Stake. Screams and hysterics from MA UBU.

Act Two

SCENE ONE

ACHRAS (*impaled*), *Ubu's* CONSCIENCE.

CONSCIENCE. Sir.

ACHRAS. Hhron.

CONSCIENCE. And so on and so forth.

ACHRAS. There must be something beyond this hhron, but what? I ought to be dead! Leave me in peace.

CONSCIENCE. Sir, although my philosophy condemns outright any form of action, what Mister Ubu has done is really too disgraceful, so I am going to disimpale you. (*He lengthens himself to the height of* ACHRAS.)

ACHRAS (*disimpaled*). I have no objection, Sir.

CONSCIENCE. Sir, and so on and so forth, I should like to have a word with you. Please sit down.

ACHRAS. Oh, but it's like this, look you, pray don't mention it. I should never be so rude as to sit down in the presence of an ethereal spirit to whom I owe my life, and besides, it's just not on.

CONSCIENCE. My inner voice and sense of justice tell me it's my duty to punish Mister Ubu. What revenge would you suggest?

ACHRAS. Hey, but it's like this, look you, I've thought about it for a long time. I shall simply unfasten the trap door into the cellar . . . hey . . . put the armchair on the edge, look you, and when the fellow, look you, comes in from his dinner, he'll bust the whole thing in, hey. And that'll make some sense, goodie-goodie!

CONSCIENCE. Justice will be done, and so forth.

SCENE TWO

The same, PA UBU. *Ubu's* CONSCIENCE *gets back into his suitcase.*

PA UBU. Hornstrumpot! You, Sir, certainly haven't stayed put as I arranged you. Well, since you're still alive to be of use to us, don't forget to tell your cook that she's in the habit of serving the soup with too much salt in it and that the joint was overdone. That's not at all the way we like them. It's not that we aren't able, by our skill in pataphysics, to make the most exquisite dishes rise from the earth, but that doesn't prevent your methods, Sir, from provoking our indignation!

ACHRAS. Oh, but it's like this, I promise you it will never happen again . . . (PA UBU *is engulfed in the trap.*)
. . . Look you . . .

PA UBU. Hornstrumpot, Sir! What is the meaning of this farce? Your floor boards are in a rotten state. We shall be obliged to make an example of you.

ACHRAS. It's only a trap door, look you.

CONSCIENCE. Mister Ubu is too fat, he'll never go through.

PA UBU. By my green candle, a trap door must be either open or shut. All the beauty of the phynancial theatre consists in the smooth functioning of its trap doors. This one is choking us, it's flaying our transverse colon and our great epiploon. Unless you extract us we shall certainly croak.

ACHRAS. All that's in my power, look you, is to charm your last moments by the reading of some of the characterclystic passages, look you, of my treatise on the habits of polyhedra, and of the thesis which I have taken sixty years to compose on the tishoos of the clonic suction. You'd rather not? Oh, very well, I'm off – I couldn't bear to watch you give up the ghost; it's quite too sad. (*Exit.*)

SCENE THREE

PA UBU, *his* CONSCIENCE.

PA UBU. My Conscience, where are you? Hornstrumpot, you certainly gave us good advice. We shall do penance and perhaps restore into your hands some small fraction of what we have taken. We shall desist from the use of our debraining machine.

CONSCIENCE. Sir, I've never wished for the death of a sinner, and so on and so forth. I offer you a helping hand.

PA UBU. Hurry up, Sir, we're dying. Pull us out of this trap door without delay and we shall accord you a full day's leave of absence from your suitcase.

Ubu's CONSCIENCE, *after releasing* UBU, *throws the suitcase in the hole.*

CONSCIENCE (*gesticulating*). Thank you, Sir. Sir, there's no better exercise than gymnastics. Ask any health expert.

PA UBU. Hornstrumpot, Sir, you play the fool too much. To show you our superiority in this, as in everything else, we are going to perform the prestidigitatious leap, which may surprise you, when you take into account the enormity of our strumpot.

He begins to run and jump.

CONSCIENCE. Sir, I entreat you, don't do anything of the sort, you'll only stove in the floor completely, and disappear down another hole. Observe our own light touch. (*He remains hanging by his feet.*) Oh! help! help! I shall rupture something, come and help me, Mister Ubu.

PA UBU (*sitting down*). Oh no. We shall do nothing of the kind, Sir. We are performing our digestive functions at this moment, and the slightest dilatation of our strumpot might instantly prove fatal. In two or three hours at the most, the digestive process will be finalized in the proper manner and we'll fly to your aid. And besides, we are by no means in the habit of unhooking such tatters off the peg.

CONSCIENCE *wriggles around, and finally falls on* UBU's *strum-pot.*

PA UBU. Ah, that's too much, Sir. We don't tolerate anyone camping about on us, and least of all, you!

Not finding the suitcase, he takes his CONSCIENCE *by the feet, opens the door of the lavatory recess at the end of the room, and shoves him head first down the drain, between the two stone footrests.*

SCENE FOUR

PA UBU; *the three* PALCONTENTS, *standing up in their packing-cases.*

THE PALCONTENTS. Those who aren't skeered of his tiny beard are all of them fools and flunk-at-schools – who'll get a surprise ere the day is out – that's what his machine is all about. For he doan' wan' – his royal person – a figure of fun – for some son-of-a-gun. – Yeh, he doan' like his little Mary – to be passed remarks on by Tom, Dick, or Harry. – This barrel that rolls, arrel that rolls, arrel that rolls is Pa Ubu.

Meanwhile, PA UBU *lights his green candle, a jet of hydrogen in the sulphurous steam, which, constructed after the principle of the Philosopher's Organ, gives out a perpetual flute note. He also hangs up two notices on the walls: 'Machine-pricking done here' and 'Get your nears cut.'*)

CRAPENTAKE. Hoy, Mister! Some folks has all the trouble. Mister Rebontier's already had eleven doses of the Bleed-Pig machine this morning in the place de la Concorde. Hoy!

BINANJITTERS. Mister, like you told me to, I've carried a case of explosive knuckle-dusters to Mister * * * * *, and a pot full of pschitt to Mister * * * * *! Hoy!

FOURZEARS. I've been in Egypt, Mister, and I've brought back that there singing Memnon. By reason of which matter, as I don't know if he roightlee has to be wound up before he sings every morning, I've deposited him in the penny bank. Hoy!

PA UBU. Silence, you clots. We are moved to meditation. The sphere is the perfect form; the sun is the perfect planet, and in us nothing is more perfect than our head, always uplifted toward the sun and aspiring to its shape – except perhaps the human eye, mirror of that star and cast in its likeness. The sphere is the form of the angels. To man is it given to be but an incomplete angel. And yet, more perfect than the cylinder, less perfect than the sphere, radiates the barrel's hyper-physical body. We, its isomorph, are passing fair.

THE PALCONTENTS. Those who aren't skeered – of his tiny beard – are all of them fools – and flunk-at-schools – who'll find themselves, ere the day is done – in his knacking-machine for their bit of fun.

PA UBU, *who was sitting at his table, gets up and walks.*

THE PALCONTENTS: This barrel that rolls, arrel that rolls, arrel that rolls, is Pa Ubu. And his strumpot huge, his trumpot huge, his rumpot huge, his umpot huge is like a . . .

PA UBU. *Non cum vacaveris, pataphysicandum est,* as Seneca has said. It would seem a matter of urgency that we get a patch inserted in our suit of homespun philosophy. *Omnia alia negligenda sunt,* it is certainly highly irreverent, *ut huic assideamus,* to employ casks and barrels for the vile business of sewage disposal, for that would constitute the grossest insult to our Master of Phynance now present as a quorum. *Cui nullum tempus vitae satis magnum est,* and so that's the reason why we have invented this instrument which we have no hesitation whatsoever in designating by the title of Pschittapump. (*He takes it from his pocket and puts it on the table.*)

THE PALCONTENTS. Hoy, Mister! Yas suh!

PA UBU. And now, as it's getting late, we shall retire to our slumbers. Ah, but I forgot! When you get back from Egypt, you will bring us some mummy-grease for our machine, although we are informed, hornstrumpot, that the animal runs very fast and is extremely difficult to capture. (*He takes his green candle and his pump and goes out.*)

SCENE FIVE

THE PALCONTENTS *sing, without moving, while the statue of* MEMNON *is erected in the middle of the stage, its base being a barrel.*

THE PALCONTENTS.
    Tremble and quake at the Lord of Phynance,
    Little bourgeois who's getting too big for his pants!
    It's too late to scream when we're skinning your arses,
    For the Palcontent's knock means he'll chop off your block
    With a sideways look through the top of his glasses . . .
    Meanwhile at dawn Pa Ubu leaves his couch,
    No sooner awake, he's a hundred rounds to make,
    With a bang he is out and flings open the door
    Where the verminous Palcontents snozzle and snore.
    He pricks up an ear, lets it down with a whistle,
    To a kick on the bum they fall in by the drum
    Till the parade ground's a mass of unmilitary gristle.
    Then he reads his marauders their bloodthirsty orders,
    Throws them a crust, betimes an onion raw,
    And with his boot inclines them through the door . . .
    With ponderous tread he quits his retinue,
    Inquires the hour, consults his clockatoo . . .
    'Great God! 'tis six! how late we are today!
    Bestir yourself, my lady wife Ubé!
    Hand me my pschittasword and money-tweezers.'
    'Oh, Sir,' says she, 'permit a wife's suggestion:
    Of washing your dear face is there no question?'
    The subject is distasteful to the Lord of Phynance
    (Sometime King of Aragon, of Poland, and of France);
    Through his foul breeks he infiltrates his braces,
    And, come rain or snow or hail, slanting to the morning gale,
    Bends his broad back toward the lonely places.

Act Three

SCENE ONE

THE PALCONTENTS *cross the stage, chanting:*

Walk with prudence, watch with care.
Show them how vigilant the Palcontents are,
Wisely discriminating how matters lie
Twixt black tycoons and honest passers-by.
Look at that one – his pin-stripe suit, his multi-coloured
   stockings, his plume of feathers – a Rentier or I'm a
   Dutchman.
Abominable countenance, cowardly sucker, we'll give you a
   thorough beating up on the spot.
In vain the Rentier tries to appease the Palcontents. He's
   loaded with fetters and belaboured with punches.
The Honourable Pa Ubu will be agreeably surprised.
He shall have Rentier's brains for dinner.

They go out.

SCENE TWO

REBONTIER, ACHRAS *enter, one from the right, the other from
the left. They recite their soliloquies simultaneously.*

REBONTIER (*dressed as a rentier, multicoloured stockings, plume
of feathers, etc.*). Ha, it's shameful! it's revolting! A miserable civil servant. I only get 3,700 francs as salary and every
morning Herr Ubu demands the payment of a treasury bill
for 80,000 francs. If I can't pay cash I have to go and get a
taste of the Bleed-Pig machine set up permanently in the
place de la Concorde, and for each session he charges me
15,000 francs. It's shameful, it's revolting.

ACHRAS. Oh, but it's like this, I've no way of staying at home.

Herr Ubu has long made his intentions clear that I should keep out, look you; and besides, saving your presence, he has installed a pschittapump, look you, in my bedroom. Oh! there's someone coming. Another Palcontent!

REBONTIER. Whom do I behold? An emissary from the Master of Phynance? Let's jolly him along. Long live Mister Ubu!

ACHRAS. Rather than risk being impaled again, I'd better agree with him, look you. Killemoff, look you! Debrain him. Off with his nears!

REBONTIER. To the Bleed-Pig! Death to Rentiers!

ACHRAS. To the Stake, look you.

They advance on each other.

REBONTIER. Help! help! murder!

ACHRAS. Ho there, help!

They collide while trying to escape from each other.

ACHRAS (*on his knees*). Mister Palcontent, spare me. I didn't do it on purpose, look you. I am a faithful supporter of Mister Ubu.

REBONTIER. It's revolting! I am a zealous defender of the Master of Phynance and Chancellor of the Excreta.

ACHRAS. Oh, but it's like this, Guv'nor, look you, are you a Fencing Master?

REBONTIER. I greatly regret, Sir, but I have not that honour.

ACHRAS. 'Cause, 'cause, look you, oh very well, if you aren't a Fencing Master, I shall hand you my card.

REBONTIER. Sir, in that case, I see no point in any further dissimulation. I am a Fencing Master.

ACHRAS. Oh very well – (*He slaps his face.*) – give me your card now, please, look you. Because I slap all fencing masters so that they are obliged to give me their card, look you, and afterward I give the fencing masters' cards to anyone who isn't a fencing master to frighten him, because I'm a man of peace myself and now that's understood, very well then!

REBONTIER. How revolting! But Sir, you provoke me in vain.

I shan't fight a duel with you; besides, it would be too un-even.

ACHRAS. As to that, look you, set your mind at rest, I shall be magnanimous in victory.

A woolidog* crosses the stage.

REBONTIER. It's infamous! This creature sent by Mister Ubu has stripped my feet of their coverings.

ACHRAS. Your multicoloured stockings and your shoes, look you. And to think that I was going to ask you to escape with me.

REBONTIER. Escape? Where to?

ACHRAS. So we can give each other satisfaction, of course, but far away from Mister Ubu.

REBONTIER. In Belgium?

ACHRAS. Or better still, look you, in Egypt. I shall pick up a pyramid or two for my collection of polyhedra. As for your slippers, look you, I'll have the cobbler from the corner come up and repair the damage.

SCENE THREE

REBONTIER, THE PALCONTENTS, MEMNON *on his barrel.*

REBONTIER *goes to sit down, and at the same moment* MEMNON *plays a prelude on his flute, since dawn is breaking.* REBONTIER *listens horrified to what follows, as he stands in front of the barrel-base. The* PALCONTENTS, *who will enter from the other side to join in the refrain, cannot see him.*

MEMNON. A cabinet-maker was I for many a long year,
Rue du Champs de Mars in All Saints' Parish;
My dear wife was a dressmaker designing lady's wear,
And the style in which we lived was pretty lavish.
Every blooming Sunday if it wasn't raining,
We'd put on our best clothes and toddle down

---

* *chien à bas de laine:* i.e. a tax collector (*chien* = subordinate employee, *bas de laine* = a stocking stuffed with coins – see *Ubu Rex*, III, 7, p. 45). [*Editor's note.*]

To join the mob who came for the Debraining,
Rue de l'Echaudé, the greatest show in town.
One, two, watch the wheels go round,
Snip, snap, the brains fly all around,
My oh my the Rentier's in a stew!

THE PALCONTENTS. *Hip hip arse-over-tip! Hurrah for Old Ubu!*

MEMNON. With our two beloved nippers, clutching us jammily
And waving paper dolls, as happy as can be,
Upstairs on the bus we're a well-adjusted family
As we roll off merrily towards the Echaudé.
Crowding to the barrier, risking broken bones,
Regardless of the blows, we push to the front row.
Then yours truly climbs up on a pile of stones
To protect my turn-ups when the claret starts to flow,
One, two, etc.

THE PALCONTENTS. *Hip hip arse-over-tip! Hurrah for Old Ubu!*

MEMNON. Soon with brains we're plastered, the old girl and me,
Our two kids lap it up and we're all jubilating
As we watch the Palcontent display his cutlery –
The first incision's made and the numbered coffins waiting.
Suddenly I notice right up by the machine
The half-familiar phiz of a chap I used to know.
Hey, there! I shout to him, So much for you, old bean!
You tried to cheat me once, am I glad to see you go!
One, two, etc.

THE PALCONTENTS. *Hip hip arse-over-tip! Hurrah for Old Ubu!*

MEMNON. A plucking at my sleeve, it's my spouse as I perceive.
Come on, you slob, she screeches, Take a crack!
Chuck a man-sized wad of dung at the lying bastard's tongue,
The Palcontent's just turned his ruddy back!
Such excellent advice won't allow me to think twice,
I summon all my courage and let fly –
An enormous lump of pschitt meant to score the winning hit,
Got the Palcontent instead full in the eye.

THE PALCONTENTS AND MEMNON. *One, two,* etc.

MEMNON. Toppled from my heap of stone, on the barrier I'm
    thrown,
  As the Palcontent turns round to see who nicked him:
  Down the hole of no return, pulped like butter in a churn,
  And The People's justice claims another victim.
  So that is what you cop for a little Sunday hop,
  Rue de l'Echaudé where necks are craning –
  You set out like a lord and they return you on a board,
  Just because you fancied a debraining.

THE PALCONTENTS AND MEMNON. *One, two, see the wheels go
    round,*
  Snip, snap, the brains fly all around,
  My oh my the Rentier's in a stew!
  Hip hip arse-over-tip! Hurrah for Old Ubu!

SCENE FOUR

The PALCONTENTS *climb back into their packing-cases on seeing
daylight.* ACHRAS *appears, followed by* SCYTOTOMILLE *carrying his signboard and an assortment of footwear on a tray.*
MEMNON *in scavenger's uniform,* REBONTIER.

ACHRAS. So out of consideration for the unities, look you, we
  have been unable to come to your shop. Make yourself at
  home here – (*He opens the door at the back.*) – in this modest
  corner, your cobbler's sign over the door, and my young
  friend will present you with his request.

REBONTIER. Master Cobbler, I'm the one who's escaping to
  Egypt with my worthy friend Mister Achras. The woolidogs
  have stripped my feet bare. I should like to obtain some
  shoes from you.

SCYTOTOMILLE. Here's an excellent article, Sir, though I
  blush to name it: speciality of the firm – the Turd-Cruncher.
  For just as no two turds are alike so does a Turd-Cruncher
  exist for every taste. These are for while they are still steam-
  ing; these are for horse dung; these are for the oldest copro-
  liths; these are for sullen cowpats; these for the innocent

meconium of a breast-fed baby; here's something special for policeman's droppings; and this pair here is for the stools of a middle-aged man.

REBONTIER. Ah, Sir! I'll take those, they'll do me very well. How much do you charge for them, Master Cobbler?

SCYTOTOMILLE. Fourteen francs, since you respect us shoe-makers.

ACHRAS. You're making a mistake, look you, not to take this pair, look you, for policeman's droppings. You'll get more wear out of them.

REBONTIER. You're quite right, Sir. Master Cobbler, I'll take the other pair. (*He starts to go.*)

SCYTOTOMILLE. But you haven't paid for them, Sir!

REBONTIER. Because I took them instead of those things of yours for the man of middle age.

SCYTOTOMILLE. But you haven't paid for them either.

ACHRAS. Because he hasn't taken them, look you.

SCYTOTOMILLE. Fair enough.

ACHRAS (*to Rebontier*). It's not a very new trick, look you; but quite good enough for an old botcher like that: he'll make it up somehow.

ACHRAS *and* REBONTIER, *ready to leave, find themselves face to face with* THE PALCONTENTS.

SCENE FIVE

The same, THE PALCONTENTS.

THE PALCONTENTS (*outside*). Walk with prudence, watch with care, *etc.*

BINANJITTERS. We must hurry up and get in, it's daylight and our packing-cases will be closed.

CRAPENTAKE. Hi there, Palcontent 3246, here's one, catch him and stuff him in your crate.

FOURZEARS. I've got you, Mister Mummy. Mister Ubu *will* be pleased.

ACHRAS. Oh, but you've got hold of the completely wrong

idea. Let me go, look you. Don't you recognize me? It's me, Mister Achras, who's been impaled once already.

REBONTIER. Sir, let me alone, this is a revolting infringement of the liberty of the individual. Besides, I'm late for my appointment with the Bleed-Pig.

CRAPENTAKE. Look out! The Big-un's getting away.

FOURZEARS. Oh! he's a lively —, that one.

Struggle.

REBONTIER. Help, Master Cobbler, and I'll pay for my shoes.

ACHRAS. After them, look you, beat them up.

SCYTOTOMILLE. I'd rather beat it myself.

A PALCONTENT *sets fire to his hair.*

What a night! I've got hair-ache.

THE PALCONTENTS. Abominable countenance, *etc.*

They roast the COBBLER, *then close the door again: a last tongue of flame shoots through the window.* ACHRAS *and* REBONTIER *are hurled into the barrel base of* MEMNON *who is himself toppled off it on to the ground, to make room for them.*

THE PALCONTENTS (*making their way out*).
   The woolidogs, those golliwogs . . .
   The money bunnies, tweezer geezers . . .
   That unfortunate rentier, Mister Rebontier,
   Is covered with pschitt from head to feet;
   While the onlookers jeer and not one spares a tear . . .
   The phynancial camels are last in his train:
   The phynancial camels . . . they've humped it in vain.

Act Four

SCENE ONE

Meanwhile, MEMNON *has picked himself up, readjusted his triple-decker cap, and his sewage-wader's topboots, and signals from the doorway.* MA UBU.

MEMNON. Sweet Mistress Ubu, you may come in – we are alone.

MA UBU. Oh my friend, I was so afraid for you when I heard all that shindy.

MEMNON. I want my barrel.

MA UBU. I don't want old Ubu.

MEMNON. We are observed. Let us continue this conversation elsewhere.

They retire to the back of the stage.

SCENE TWO

The same, in the lavatory recess in the back, the door of which remains half open. VOICE OF PA UBU *and* THE PALCONTENTS *off-stage.*

VOICE OF UBU. Hornstrumpot! We've taken possession of Mister Achras's phynance, we've impaled him and commandeered his home, and in this home, stung by remorse, we are looking for somewhere where we can return to him the very tangible remains of what we have stolen – to wit, his dinner.

VOICES OF THE PALCONTENTS. In a great box of stainless steel . . .

MA UBU. It's Mister Ubu. I'm lost!

MEMNON. Through this diamond-shaped opening I see his

horns shining in the distance. Where can I hide? Ah, in there.

MA UBU. Don't even think of it, dear child, you'll kill yourself!

MEMNON. Kill myself? By Gog and Magog, one can live, one can breathe down there. It's all part of my job. One, two, hop!

SCENE THREE

The same, CONSCIENCE.

CONSCIENCE (*coming out like a worm at the same moment as* MEMNON *dives in*). Ow! what a shock! my head is booming from it!

MEMNON. Like an empty barrel.

CONSCIENCE. Doesn't yours boom?

MEMNON. Not in the least.

CONSCIENCE. Like a cracked pot. I'm keeping my eye on it.

MEMNON. More like an eye at the bottom of a chamber pot.

CONSCIENCE. I have in fact the honour to be the Conscience of Mister Ubu.

MEMNON. Was it he who precipitated Your Shapelessness into this hole?

CONSCIENCE. I deserved it. I tormented him and he has punished me.

MA UBU. Poor young man . . .

VOICES OF THE PALCONTENTS (*coming nearer and nearer*). Ears to the wind, without surprise . . .'

MEMNON. That's why you must go back again, and me too, and Madam Ubu as well.

They descend.

THE PALCONTENTS (*behind the door*): We get our eats through platinum teats . . .

PA UBU. Enter, hornstrumpot!

They all rush in.

SCENE FOUR

THE PALCONTENTS, *carrying green candles.* PA UBU, *in a nightshirt.*

PA UBU (*he squats down without a word. The whole thing collapses. He emerges again, thanks to the Archimedean principle. Then, with great simplicity and dignity, his nightshirt perhaps a shade darker*). Is the pschittapump out of order? Answer me or I'll have you debrained!

SCENE FIVE

The same, MEMNON *showing his head.*

MEMNON'S HEAD. It's not functioning at all, it's broken down. What a dirty business, like your debraining machine. I'm not afraid of that. It all proves my point – there's nothing like a sewage barrel. In falling in and popping out again you've done more than half the work for me.

PA UBU. By my green candle, I'll gouge your eyes out – barrel, pumpkin, refuse of humanity! (*He shoves him back, then shuts himself in the lavatory recess with* THE PALCONTENTS.)

Act Five

SCENE ONE

ACHRAS, REBONTIER.

REBONTIER. Sir, I have just witnessed a most extraordinary incident.

ACHRAS. And I think, look you, Sir, that I've seen exactly the same. No matter, go on telling me about it, and we'll try to find the explanation.

REBONTIER. Sir, I saw the customs officers at the Gare de Lyon opening a packing case to be delivered to – whom do you think?

ACHRAS. I believe I heard someone say that it was addressed to a Mister Ubu at the rue de l'Echaudé.

REBONTIER. Precisely, Sir, and inside were a man and a stuffed monkey.

ACHRAS. A large monkey?

REBONTIER. What do you mean by a large monkey? Simians are always fairly small, and can be recognized by their dark coats and collars of fur of a lighter colour. Great height is an indication of the soul's aspiration to heaven.

ACHRAS. It's the same with flies, look you. But shall I tell you what I think? I'm inclined to believe they were mummies.

REBONTIER. Egyptian mummies?

ACHRAS. Yes, Sir, that's the explanation. There was one that looked like a crocodile, look you, dried up, the skull depressed as in primitive man; the other, look you, had the brow of a thinker, and a most dignified air, ah yes, his hair and beard were white as snow.

REBONTIER. Sir, I don't know what you're driving at. Besides, the mummies, including the dignified old monkey, jumped out of their case amid a chorus of yells from the customs men and, to the consternation of the onlookers, took the tram that crosses the pont de l'Alma.

ACHRAS. Great heavens! how astonishing, we too just came here by that conveyance or, look you, for the sake of accuracy, that tramway.

REBONTIER. That's exactly what I said to myself, Sir. It's most peculiar that we did not meet them.

SCENE TWO

The same, PA UBU *opens the door, illuminated by* THE PALCONTENTS.

PA UBU. Ah-ha! Hornstrumpot! (*To* ACHRAS:) You, Sir, bugger off. You've been told to before.

ACHRAS. Oh, but it's like this, look you. This happens to be my home.

PA UBU. Horn of Ubu, Mister Rebontier, it's you, I don't doubt any longer, who came to my house to cuckold me, who mistakes my virtuous wife, in other words, for a piss-pot. We shall find ourselves, one fine day, thanks to you, the father of an archaeopteryx or worse, which won't look at all like us! Basically, we are of the opinion that cuckoldry implies marriage and therefore a marriage without cuckoldry has no validity. But for form's sake we have decided to punish him severely. Palcontents, knock him down for me!

THE PALCONTENTS *belabour* REBONTIER.

Lights, please, and you, Sir, answer me. Am I a cuckold?

REBONTIER. Owowow, owowowow!

PA UBU. How disgusting. He can't reply because he fell on his head. His brain has doubtless received an injury to the Broca convolution, where the faculty of holding forth resides. This convolution is the third frontal convolution on the left as you go in. Ask the hall-porter. . . . Excuse me, gentlemen, ask any philosopher: 'This dissolution of the mind is caused by an atrophy which little by little invades the cerebral cortex, then the grey matter, producing a fatty degeneration and atheroma of the cells, tubes, and capillaries of the nerve-substance!'* There's nothing to be done with him. We'll

* Th. Ribot: *Maladies de la Mémoire*, p. 93. [Author's note.]

have to make do with twisting the nose and nears, with re-
moval of the tongue and extraction of the teeth, laceration of
the posterior, hacking to pieces of the spinal marrow and the
partial or total spaghettification of the brain through the
heels. He shall first be impaled, then beheaded, then finally
drawn and quartered. After which the gentleman will be
free, through our great clemency, to go and get himself
hanged anywhere he chooses. No more harm will come to
him, for I wish to treat him well.

THE PALCONTENTS. Hoy, Mister!

PA UBU. Hornstrumpot! I forgot to consult my Conscience.

He goes back into the lavatory recess. Meanwhile REBONTIER
escapes, THE PALCONTENTS *howling and screaming at his heels.*
PA UBU *reappears, leading his* CONSCIENCE *by the hand.*

SCENE THREE

ACHRAS, PA UBU, *his* CONSCIENCE.

PA UBU (*to* ACHRAS). Hornstrumpot, Sir! So you refuse to
bugger off. Like my Conscience here, whom I can't get rid
of.

CONSCIENCE. Sir, don't make fun of Epictetus in his misfortune.

PA UBU. The stickabeatus is doubtless an ingenious instrument,
but the play has gone on quite long enough and we are in no
disposition to employ it today.

With a noise like an engine-whistle THE CROCODILE *crosses the
stage.*

SCENE FOUR

The same, THE CROCODILE.

ACHRAS. Oh, but it's like this, look you, what on earth is that?

PA UBU. It's a boidie.

CONSCIENCE. It's a most characteristic reptile and moreover

(*touching it*) its hands possess all the properties of a snake's.

PA UBU. Then it must be a whale, for the whale is the most in-flated boidie in existence and this animal seems thoroughly distended.

CONSCIENCE. I tell you it's a snake.

PA UBU. That should prove to Mister Conscience his stupidity and absurdity. We had come to the same conclusion long before he said so: in fact it *is* a snake! A rattler into the bargain.

ACHRAS (*Smelling it*). Poo! One thing's quite certain, look you, it ain't no polyhedron.

Ubu Enchained

(Ubu Enchaîné)

Five Acts

Translated by Simon Watson Taylor

To the several MASTERS
who acknowledged
his sovereignty while he was king
UBU ENCHAINED
offers the homage of
his shackles

PA UBU. – Hornstrumpot! We shall not have suceeded in demolishing everything unless we demolish the ruins as well. But the only way I can see of doing that is to use them to put up a lot of fine, well-designed buildings.

CHARACTERS

PA UBU

MA UBU

THE THREE FREE MEN

PISSWEET, Their Corporal

PISSALE

ELEUTHERIA

JUDGE

COURT USHER

CLERK OF THE COURT

PUBLIC PROSECUTOR

DEFENCE COUNSEL

THREE PIOUS OLD MAIDS

BROTHER BUNG

POLICEMEN

WRECKERS

GAOLER

SOLIMAN, Sultan of the Turks

SOLIMAN'S VIZIER

LORD CORNHOLER

JACK, his Valet

GUARDS

CONVICTS

LEADER OF THE CONVICTS

PEOPLE

Ubu Enchaîné remained unperformed until 1937, when it was presented at the Théâtre de la Comédie des Champs-Elysées, Paris, in a production directed by Sylvain Itkine, with sets designed by Max Ernst and music composed by Frédéric O'Brady.

This translation was first performed by the Traverse Theatre Club, Edinburgh, on September 1st, 1967 with the following cast:

PA UBU	Ian Trigger
MA UBU	Miriam Margolyes
THE THREE FREE MEN	William Simons
	David Wood
	Toby Salaman
PISSWEET, their Corporal	Christopher Serle
PISSALE	Brian Walton
ELEUTHERIA	Hildegard Neil
JUDGE	David Wood
PUBLIC PROSECUTOR	William Simons
DEFENCE COUNSEL	Toby Salaman

THREE PIOUS OLD MAIDS	William Simons
	David Wood
	Toby Salaman
BROTHER BUNG	Ian Mandleberg
GAOLER	Ian Mandleberg
SOLIMAN, Sultan of the Turks	Christopher Serle
SOLIMAN'S VIZIER	Brian Walton
LORD CORNHOLER	Christopher Serle
JACK, his Valet	Brian Walton
CONVICTS	William Simons
	David Wood
	Toby Salaman

POLICEMEN, WRECKERS, PEOPLE

Directed by Gordon McDougall
Designed by Gerald Scarfe
Lighting by André Tammas
Effects by Ivor Davies
Music and special lighting effects by Mark Boyle and The Soft
    Machine.

This translation was adapted for radio by Martin Esslin and
first broadcast on the BBC Third Programme in July 1968.

Act One

SCENE ONE

PA UBU, MA UBU.

PA UBU *comes forward and says nothing*.

MA UBU. What! You say nothing, Pa Ubu! Surely you haven't forgotten the Word?

PA UBU. Psch . . . aw, Ma Ubu! I don't want to say that word any longer, it got me into too much trouble.

MA UBU. What do you mean – trouble? The throne of Poland, the great bonnet, the umbrella . . .

PA UBU. I don't care for the umbrella any longer, Ma Ubu, it's too hard to handle. I shall just use my science of physics to stop it raining!

MA UBU. Fathead! . . . The property of the nobles confiscated, the taxes collected three times over, my own inspiring presence at your awakening in the bear's cave, the free ride on the ship which brought us back to France where, by pronouncing the glorious Word, you can be appointed Master of Phynances whenever you choose! We're in France now, Pa Ubu, this is hardly the moment for you to forget how to speak French.

PA UBU. Hornstrumpot, Ma Ubu, I spoke French while we were in Poland, but that didn't stop young Boggerlas from ripping open my boodle, did it, or Captain M'Nure from betraying me most shamefully, or the Tsar from scaring my phynance charger by his stupidity in letting himself fall into a ditch, or the enemy from shooting at our august person despite our instructions to the contrary, or the bear from rending our Palcontents asunder even though we addressed the savage beast in Latin from on top of our rock, or indeed, you, madam our spouse, from dilapidating our treasures and even filching our phynance charger's dollar a day fodder allowance!

MA UBU. You should forget such minor setbacks. What will we

live on if you no longer want to be Master of Phynances or king?

PA UBU. By the work of our hands, Ma Ubu!

MA UBU. What, Pa Ubu, you intend to beat up the passers-by and rob them?

PA UBU. Oh no, they'd only hit me back! I want to be kind to the passers-by, useful to them, in fact I want to work for the passers-by, Ma Ubu. Now that we are in the land where liberty is equal to fraternity, and fraternity more or less means the equality of legality, and since I am incapable of behaving like everyone else and since being the same as everyone else is all the same to me seeing that I shall certainly end up by killing everyone else, I might as well become a slave, Ma Ubu!

MA UBU. A slave! But you're too fat, Pa Ubu!

PA UBU. All the better for doing a fat lot of work. You, madam our female, go and set out our slave apron, and our unmentionable slave brush, and our slave hook, and our slave's shoe-polishing kit. But as for yourself, stay just as you are, so that everyone can see plainly that you are wearing your beautiful costume of slave cook!

SCENE TWO

The Parade Ground. The THREE FREE MEN, *their* CORPORAL.

THREE FREE MEN. We are the Free Men and this is our Corporal. – Three cheers for freedom, rah, rah, rah! We are free. – Let's not forget, it's our duty to be free. Hey! not so fast, or we might arrive on time. Freedom means never arriving on time – never, never! – for our freedom drills. Let's disobey together . . . No! not together: one, two, three! the first will disobey on the count of one, the second on two, the third on three. That makes all the difference. Let's each march out of step with the other two, however exhausting it may be to keep it up. Let's disobey individually – here comes the corporal of the Free Men!

CORPORAL. Fall in!

They fall out.

You, Free Man number three, you get two days' detention for being in line with number two. The training-manual lays down quite clearly that you must be free! – Individual drills in disobedience . . . Blind and unwavering indiscipline at all times constitutes the real strength of all Free Men. – Slope . . . arms!

THREE FREE MEN. Let's talk in the ranks. – Let's disobey. – The first on the count of one, the second on the count of two, the third on the count of three. – One, two, three!

CORPORAL. As you were! Number one, you should have grounded arms; number two, surrendered your weapon; number three thrown your rifle six paces behind you and then tried to strike a libertarian attitude. Fall out! One, two! one two!

They fall in and then march off, being careful not to march in step.

SCENE THREE

PA UBU, MA UBU.

MA UBU. Oh! Pa Ubu, how handsome you look in your cap and apron. Now go and find some Free Man and try out your hook and your shoe-polishing brush on him, so that you can start off in your new duties right away.

PA UBU. Ah ha! I can see three or four specimens scurrying off over there.

MA UBU. Catch one, Pa Ubu.

PA UBU. Hornstrumpot! I shall be delighted to do so. Polishing of the feet, cutting of the hair, singeing of the moustaches, forcing of the little wooden pick into the nearoles . . .

MA UBU. Hey, are you out of your mind, Pa Ubu! You must imagine you're still King of Poland.

PA UBU. Madam my female, I know exactly what I'm doing, and you – you don't know what you're talking about. When I was king I did all that for my further glory and for Poland; but now I'm going to institute a modest price-list and they'll have to pay me: twisting of the nose, for instance, will cost three francs twenty-five. For an even smaller sum I'll beat you up with your own egg-whisk.

MA UBU *flees.*

Let us follow these people, in any case, and offer them our services.

SCENE FOUR

PA UBU, *the* CORPORAL, *the* THREE FREE MEN. *The* CORPORAL *and the* FREE MEN *march up and down for some time; then* PA UBU *falls into step with them.*

CORPORAL. Slope . . . arms!

PA UBU *obeys with his unmentionable brush.*

PA UBU. Hurrah for the Pschittanarmy!
CORPORAL. Halt! Halt! Or rather, no! Disobey by not halting!

The FREE MEN *halt,* PA UBU *steps forward from the ranks.*

Who is this new recruit, freer than any of you, who has invented an arms drill I've never seen before in all the seven years I've been ordering 'Slope . . . arms!'?
PA UBU. We obeyed the command, Sir, in order to carry out our slavish duties. I have performed the motions of 'slope arms'.
CORPORAL. I've explained this piece of drill time and time again, but this is the first time I've ever seen it done properly. Your theoretical knowledge of freedom is greater than mine, since you even go so far as to obey commands. You are the greatest Free Man of us all. Your name, Sir?
PA UBU. Herr Ubu, sometime King of Poland and Aragon, Count of Mondragon, Count of Sandomir, Marquis of Saint-Gregory. At present, slave, at your service, Mister . . . ?
CORPORAL. Pissweet . . . Corporal of the Free Men . . . but, when ladies are present, the Marquis of Grandmeadow. Please remember, I beg you, to address me only by my title,

even if you should find yourself in command over me, which seems likely, since I can tell from your knowledge of the Freedom training-manual that you must be a sergeant at least.

PA UBU. Corporal Pissweet, we shall remember, Sir. But I have come to this country to be a slave, not to give orders, although it is true that I was in fact a sergeant once, when I was a little boy, and even a captain of dragoons. Corporal Pissweet, farewell.

He marches off.

CORPORAL. Farewell, Count of Saint-Gregory. – Squad, halt!

The FREE MEN *march across the stage and exeunt.*

SCENE FIVE

ELEUTHERIA, PISSALE.

PISSALE. Eleutheria, my dear, I'm afraid we are rather late.

ELEUTHERIA. Uncle Pissale . . .

PISSALE. Never call me that, even when there's no one around! Marquis of Grandair – a far simpler name, you will agree, and one which when pronounced does not make people turn round and stare. You could at least address me simply as 'uncle'.

ELEUTHERIA. Uncle, it really doesn't matter if we are late. Since you got me this job . . .

PISSALE. Through my important connections.

ELEUTHERIA. . . . as canteen-girl to the Free Men, I have memorized a few of the rules in their Freedom training-manual. I arrive late, so they don't get anything to drink, so they're thirsty and understand all the better how useful it is to have a canteen-girl.

PISSALE. In fact they never see you at all. It would be more sensible if you stopped coming altogether and so saved your uncle from being roasted by the hot sun on this parade ground every day.

ELEUTHERIA. Uncle Piss ... I mean, uncle, why don't you
simply stay at home then?

PISSALE. That would not be proper, niece. You are a young
girl, Eleutheria, and I must keep an eye on the Free Men to
see that they don't take too many liberties with you. A per-
missive uncle is a living scandal. You are not a free ...
woman, you are my niece. I have already arranged, with
great ingenuity, that although it is the custom in this land
of the free to go naked, in your case your decolletage is con-
fined to your feet ...

ELEUTHERIA. So that's why you never buy me shoes!

PISSALE. Besides, I'm less worried about the Free Men than I
am about your fiancé, the Marquis of Grandmeadow.

ELEUTHERIA. And yet you're giving a ball in his honour this
evening ... Oh, uncle, hasn't he got a gorgeous name!

PISSALE. And that is why, dear child, I must remind you once
again that, in his presence, it is unseemly for you to call
me ...

ELEUTHERIA. Pissale – no, I won't forget, uncle.

SCENE SIX

The same. PA UBU.

PA UBU. Those soldiers don't seem to have much cash, so I'd
better look for someone else to serve. Ah! here comes a
charming maiden carrying a green silk parasol, accompanied
by a respectable-looking gentleman wearing a red ribbon in
his button-hole. Let us endeavour not to alarm them. –
Hornstrumpot! by my green candle, sweet child, I take the
liberty – your liberty – of offering you my services. Twisting
of the nose, extraction of the brain ... no, no, I forgot; I
meant to say: polishing of the feet.

ELEUTHERIA. Leave me alone.

PISSALE. You must be dreaming, Sir! Can't you see she's
barefoot?

SCENE SEVEN

The same. MA UBU.

PA UBU. Ma Ubu! bring me the polishing-hook and the polishing-box and the polishing-brush, and come here and get a good grip on her feet! (*To* PISSALE.) As for you, Sir! . . .

ELEUTHERIA }
PISSALE   } Help!

MA UBU (*running up*). Here you are, Pa Ubu, I obey you. But what do you intend to do with your polishing kit? She's not wearing shoes.

PA UBU. I intend to polish her feet with this special foot-polishing brush. I am a slave, hornstrumpot! No one shall prevent me from performing my slavish duty. I shall serve pitilessly. Killemoff, debrain!

MA UBU *holds* ELEUTHERIA *by the ankles.* PA UBU *hurls himself upon* PISSALE.

MA UBU. What senseless brutality! Now she's fainted.

PISSALE (*collapsing*). And I'm dead!

PA UBU (*polishing away vigorously*). I knew I'd be able to make them keep quiet. I can't stand people making a din! Well, now that job's done I can claim the fee that I have earned honestly with the sweat of my brow.

MA UBU. Better revive her, so she can pay you.

PA UBU. Oh no! She'd probably want to give me a tip, and all I demand is a fair price for my work. Besides, to be quite fair I'd also have to resuscitate that old fool I've just massacred, and that would take too long. In any case, as a conscientious slave I am bound to anticipate her slightest wish. Ah! here's the young lady's purse and the gentleman's wallet. Into my pocket with them!

MA UBU. You're keeping it all, Pa Ubu?

PA UBU. You don't think I'm going to squander the fruits of

my labours buying you presents, do you, you stupid old bag?
(*Counting the banknotes.*) Fifty francs . . . fifty francs . . . a
thousand francs . . . (*Reading a card.*) Corporal Pissale,
Marquis of Grandair.

MA UBU. I mean, aren't you going to leave them anything,
Mister Ubu, Sir?

PA UBU. Ma Ubu! I'm gonna black both yer eyes, then exorbi-
tate them! Besides, this purse only contains fourteen gold
pieces, all with a female figure on one side symbolizing
Freedom.

ELEUTHERIA *regains consciousness and tries to escape.*

And now go and find a carriage, Ma Ubu.

MA UBU. Miserable creature! Can't you even summon up the
energy to make your getaway on foot?

PA UBU. No, I need a large coach in which to install this charming child, and see her safely home.

MA UBU. Pa Ubu, you're just not being logical. Are you getting
senile, turning into an honest man like this, and taking pity
on your victims? You must be off your rocker! And how
about this corpse, sprawled on the ground for all to see, are
you just going to leave it here?

PA UBU. Bah! I'm getting rich . . . as usual. I shall carry on
with my work as a slave. Come on, let's stuff her in the
carriage . . .

MA UBU. But what about Pissale's corpse?

PA UBU. Into the boot of the carriage. Good. Now all evidence
of the crime has vanished. You get in with her to act as her
nurse, cook and chaperone, and I'll climb up into the driver's
box at the back.

MA UBU (*bringing in the coach*). Will you eventually be rigged
out in beautiful white stockings and a gold-embroidered
coat, Pa Ubu?

PA UBU. Indeed I shall. I have certainly earned them with my
zeal. On second thoughts, since I don't have them yet, *I* shall
accompany the young lady inside and *you* can perch up there
at the back.

MA UBU. But Pa Ubu . . .
PA UBU. Up you get, and off we go!

He gets in with ELEUTHERIA.
The coach rumbles off.

Act Two

SCENE ONE

Inside the coach. PA UBU, ELEUTHERIA.

PA UBU. Sweet child, in me you behold the most devoted of your slaves. Vouchsafe me just one word, I beg ... one word, hornstrumpot! that I may know you appreciate my services.

ELEUTHERIA. That wouldn't be at all proper, sir. I must follow my uncle Pissale's instructions, never to allow any man to take liberties with me except in his presence.

PA UBU. Ah! your uncle Pissale? Don't let that bother you, sweet child, we had the foresight to bring him along with us in the boot of this vehicle!

He hauls out PISSALE's *corpse and brandishes it in front of* ELEUTHERIA *who promptly faints*

By my green candle, this young person has mistaken our virtuous intentions. Seduction would, in any case, be impossible at this moment since we have taken the precaution not only of securing the person of the uncle but also of hoisting our dearly-beloved Ma Ubu on to the back of the vehicle to keep a look-out, and she would most certainly rupture our gutbag if she caught us at it! We are simply petitioning this young lady humbly for the post of lackey! After all, her uncle didn't raise any objection to the idea a moment ago. And so, hornstrumpot, when I get this lady home I'm determined to stand guard outside her door while Ma Ubu lavishes her attentions upon her, seeing as how she faints so often. No matter who knocks and asks to see her, I'll not let them in. I shall immure her, day in day out, in the prison of my services. I shall never let her out of my sight. Hurrah for slavery!

SCENE TWO

The hallway of PISSALE'*s house.* PA UBU, MA UBU.

MA UBU. Someone's ringing, Pa Ubu.

PA UBU. Hornphynance! it's doubtless our faithful mistress. As we all know, sensible dog-owners tie little bells around their pets' necks so that they won't get run over, and to prevent accidents bicyclists are required by law to announce their presence by ringing a bell loud enough to be heard fifty feet away. Similarly, the faithfulness of a master can be judged by his ringing non-stop for fifty minutes. He simply means: 'I am here, take it easy, I'm looking after things during your time off.'

MA UBU. But after all, Pa Ubu, you are her man-servant, her cook and her head-waiter. Perhaps she's hungry, and is trying discreetly to draw your benevolent attention to the fact of her existence, so as to find out if you've given the order for Madam to be served.

PA UBU. Madam is not served, Ma Ubu! Madam will be served in our own good time, when we have finished our own meal, and then only if a few scraps of food should still happen to remain on our table!

MA UBU. Well, how about offering her the unmentionable brush?

PA UBU. No, I don't use it much any longer. It was all right so long as I was king because it amused all the little children. But we have grown wiser since then, and have discovered that what makes little children laugh may very well frighten grown-ups. Now, by my green candle, this endless ringing is intolerable! We are perfectly well aware that Madam is there; a well-trained employer should know better than to kick up such a racket at a moment when we are off-duty.

MA UBU. If there's nothing left to eat, perhaps you could offer her something to drink, Pa Ubu?

PA UBU. Hornstrumpot! If that will make her shut up we will have that great kindness!

*He stamps down to the cellar in a rage, and brings up a dozen
bottles, making several trips to do so.*

MA UBU. Help! I knew he was going crazy! a stingy creature
like him offering her a dozen bottles! And where on earth
did he dig them up? I thought I'd drunk the last drop myself.

PA UBU. There you are, madam our wife. Go and bear witness
to our mistress of our attentiveness and generosity. I hope
that by carefully draining these empty objects you will
accumulate enough dregs to be able to offer her a glass of
wine with our compliments.

MA UBU, *reassured, begins to obey. An enormous spider escapes
from one of the empty bottles.* MA UBU *flees, uttering piercing
screams.* PA UBU *seizes the beast and puts it in his snuff-box.*

SCENE THREE

ELEUTHERIA's *room.* ELEUTHERIA, *the corpse of* PISSALE.

ELEUTHERIA. Help! horrors! Rather than remain alone with a
corpse, I see no choice but to ring for that dreadful couple
who have forced themselves upon me as servants. (*She
rings.*) No one answers. Perhaps they didn't have the effron-
tery to move into the house of their unfortunate victim. Disgusting Pa Ubu! That horrible wife of his! (*She rings again.*)
No one! Ah, unhappy Pissale! My uncle, my dear uncle!
Uncle Pissale!

PISSALE (*sitting up*). Marquis of Grandair, dear child!

ELEUTHERIA. Eek! (*She faints.*)

PISSALE. Oh, so now *she's* playing dead! Ah well! that's life.
Oh, poor little Eleutheria!

ELEUTHERIA. Did you speak to me, uncle?

PISSALE. Hah, you've regained consciousness?

ELEUTHERIA. Why, uncle P . . . p . . . please tell me why you
aren't dead any longer?

PISSALE. What's all this p . . . p . . . p . . . p . . . please?

ELEUTHERIA. Marquis of Grandair. I almost said Pissale by mistake.

PISSALE. I'll forgive you, my dear. In fact I wasn't dead at all. I was simply carrying to its logical conclusion my method of accompanying you everywhere as unobtrusively as possible and taking part in all your activities purely by virtue of being your uncle.

ELEUTHERIA. So that's why you arrived home in the boot of the carriage! Well, since you are not dead after all I hope I can count on your valour and resolution to eject this dreadful Pa Ubu and his equally dreadful wife from my house?

PISSALE. I don't see any point in that, since it so happens that I have just involuntarily paid them several months' salary in advance. They are fine servants, and they learn fast, too: why, the first thing Pa Ubu did was to read over my papers and learn my title by heart – 'Marquis of Grandair, Marquis of Grandair' he kept repeating! Tonight, at the party to celebrate your engagement to the Marquis of Grandmeadow, I intend to have Pa Ubu announce all the guests.

ELEUTHERIA. But the Ubes never obey! (*She rings.*)

PISSALE. Then what's the point of ringing for them? You hate the sight of them. They are excellent servants, niece, I assure you, but if you're so determined to have someone throw them out of the house you may as well leave the job to Corporal the Marquis of Grandmeadow this evening: he's used to giving orders to professional disobeyers. He's been invited to attend the ball in uniform, and in any case his squad of Free Men provides an additional uniform for him on a hierarchical level.

SCENE FOUR

The Hallway. PA UBU, MA UBU.

PA UBU (*calmly*). They're still ringing.

MA UBU. That's not Madam ringing now. She must have got it into her head at last that we aren't at home, or at least aren't taking orders today. That was the doorbell.

PA UBU. The doorbell, Ma Ubu? Ah, let us not in our zeal for slavedom neglect our functions as slave-porter. Bolt the door, put up the iron bars, close all twelve locks and make sure that the little pot of you-know-what is positioned in the window just above the front door, brim-full and ready to greet any visitors standing underneath.

MA UBU. The bell-cord's been ripped out by now, but whoever it is is banging on the door. It must be a most distinguished visitor.

PA UBU. Oh well, Ma Ubu, you'd better fasten the end of our chain of office to the iron ring in the wall over there, and hang over the staircase that venerable sign which reads: BEWARE OF THE DOG. If these people have the audacity to force their way in, I shall bite them savagely and tread on their toes too.

SCENE FIVE

The same. PISSWEET *breaks down the door. Grotesque battle with the* UBES *ensues.*

PISSWEET. Slave! . . . Ha, *you*, sergeant of the Free Men, a servant here? Well, then, announce the Marquis of Grand-meadow.

PA UBU. Madam has gone out, Mister Pissweet. Or, to be more exact, this is not one of the days when we permit her to receive company. I forbid you to see her.

PISSWEET. This is an excellent occasion to prove that I know my theory of indiscipline by heart. I'm not only coming in, I'm going to give you a thorough thrashing into the bargain! (*He takes a dog-whip out of his pocket and brandishes it.*)

PA UBU. Ooh, a whip, do you see that, Ma Ubu? I've been promoted: foot-polisher, lackey, porter, and now a whipped slave. Soon I'll be in gaol, and if God grants me life I'll end up in the galleys. Our fortune is made, Ma Ubu!

PISSWEET. This is going to be quite a job, beating him all over that huge surface!

PA UBU. Ah, what a triumph! See how this lash obeys all the

curves of my strumpot. Why, I'm as good as a snake-charmer.

MA UBU. You look more like a whipping-top spinning round, Pa Ubu.

PISSWEET. Phew! I'm worn out. Now, Pa Ubu, I order you to announce me to your mistress.

PA UBU. First of all, who are you to give orders? Only slaves give orders here. What, pray, is your rank in slavery?

PISSWEET. *Me* – a corporal, a soldier – slave? I'm a slave only to love. Eleutheria, future Marquise of Grandmeadow, the lovely canteen-girl of the Free Men, is not only my fiancée but in fact my *mistress*, so to speak.

PA UBU. Hornstrumpot, sir! I never thought of that. I'm slave-of-all-work here: thank you for reminding me of my respon-sibilities. That particular service is all part of my duties, and I shall accomplish it expeditiously, to save you the trouble yourself . . .

MA UBU. Hey! you big ninny! what do you think you're up to?

PA UBU. This gentleman, *who happens to be free*, will take my place at your side, sweet child.

Exit PA UBU, *up the stairs, hotly pursued by* MA UBU *and* PISSWEET.

SCENE SIX

PISSALE's *house: the ball in full swing.* ELEUTHERIA, PISSALE, PA UBU, MA UBU. PA UBU *is waltzing with* ELEUTHERIA.

ELEUTHERIA. Help, help! Uncle, protect me!

PISSALE. As your uncle, it goes without saying that I'll do everything I can.

MA UBU (*running up, shaking her fists in the air*). Pa Ubu, Pa Ubu, hey, stop waltzing in that ridiculous way! You've gobbled up all the refreshments from the buffet-table and you're smeared with jam from eyebrow to elbow. You've slung your dancing-partner under your arm, stupid, and since you don't have the corporal's whip any longer to help you spin round you're bound to fall on your strumpot any moment now!

PA UBU (*to* ELEUTHERIA). Ah, sweet child, how we revel in these worldly pleasures! I had every intention of fulfilling my domestic duties by announcing the guests, but there weren't any. – Well, they told me to announce them but they didn't tell me to let them in; and as for serving the refreshments, there I was, behind the table, eager to help, but since no one arrived I had no choice but to eat everything up myself! And now, hornstrumpot, it is someone's duty to ask you to dance! So, by my green candle, I am performing that service; at least there will be that much less floor-space for Ma Ubu to have to polish afterwards!

They waltz.

SCENE SEVEN

The same. PISSWEET *and the* FREE MEN *burst in.*

PISSWEET. Don't touch that man! I'm going to slay him personally! Don't arrest him!

THREE FREE MEN. All disobey! No, not together! One, two, three! (*To* PA UBU.) Off to prison, to prison, to prison, hey?

They drag him off, with PISSWEET *in the lead.*

ELEUTHERIA (*throws herself into the arms of* PISSALE). Oh, Uncle Pissale!

PISSALE. Marquis of Grandair, dear child.

MA UBU (*running after* PA UBU). Hey, Pa Ubu, I've always shared your bad luck, so now I follow you loyally in your good fortune!

Act Three

SCENE ONE

A prison. PA UBU, MA UBU.

PA UBU. Hornphynance! at last we're beginning to look well-dressed. They've exchanged our livery, which was in any case rather tight across our bumboozle, for this exquisite grey uniform. Why, we might almost be back in Poland!

MA UBU. Yes, we're well housed here, I'd say it's just as comfortable as the palace of Wenceslas. And nobody rings or breaks doors here.

PA UBU. Ah, how right you are! The trouble with the houses in this country is that the front doors can't be locked and people shoot in and out like wind through the sails of a windmill. But I have had the foresight to order this particular building to be fortified by strong iron doors and by solid bars at all the windows. And the Masters obey our instructions punctiliously by bringing our meals to us twice a day. What's more, we have made use of our knowledge of physics to invent an ingenious device whereby the rain drips through the roof every morning, so that the straw in our cell may remain sufficiently moist.

MA UBU. But, Pa Ubu, now that we're in here we can't leave again, can we?

PA UBU. Leave here! I've had quite enough of marching at the tail of my armies across the Ukraine. Hornstrumpot, I'll never budge again! From now on, people will have to come and see *me*. And certain small domestic beasts are permitted to regard our person on specific days of the week.

SCENE TWO

The Great Hall of Justice. PA UBU, MA UBU, PISSWEET, PISSALE, ELEUTHERIA, JUDGE, LAWYERS, CLERK, USHER, GUARDS, PEOPLE.

PA UBU. We observe with pleasure, gentlemen, the fact that all the wheels of justice have been set in motion in our honour, that our guards have had the forethought to wear their special moustaches – the ones well-stained with the evidence of banquets and Sunday dinners – in order to endow the bench of our infamy with greater prestige, and that our liege subjects are listening attentively and remaining silent!

USHER. Silence in court!

MA UBU. Psst! Shut up, Pa Ubu, or you'll get yourself thrown out.

PA UBU. Certainly not, there are guards here specially to keep me from leaving. And I am obliged to talk incessantly, since all these people are here specifically for the purpose of interrogating me. – And now, produce those persons who have lodged a complaint against us!

THE JUDGE. Bring forward the accused and his accomplice!

They are hustled up, aided by a few kicks and thumps.

Your name, prisoner?

PA UBU. Francis Ubu, sometime king of Poland and of Aragon, doctor of pataphysics, Count of Mondragon, Count of Sandomir, Marquis of Saint-Gregory.

PISSWEET. Alias: Pa Ubu!

MA UBU. Victorine Ubu, sometime queen of Poland.

PISSALE. Alias: Ma Ubu!

CLERK (*writing*). Pa Ubu and Ma Ubu.

JUDGE. Accused, what's your age?

PA UBU. I'm not quite sure. I gave it to Ma Ubu to keep a long time ago – so long ago, in fact, that she's not only lost it but her own age as well.

MA UBU. Ill-bred lout!

PA UBU. Madam, psch . . . No, I've sworn not to use the Word any longer: it might bring me luck and get me acquitted, and I'm determined to end up in the galleys.

JUDGE (*to the plaintiffs*). Your names?

PISSALE. Marquis of Grandair.

PA UBU (*angrily*). Alias: Pissale!

CLERK (*writing*). Pissale, and his niece Eleutheria Pissale.

ELEUTHERIA. Oh dear! Uncle!

PISSALE. Calm yourself, niece, I'm still your uncle.

PISSWEET. Marquis of Grandmeadow.

MA UBU (*angrily*). Alias: Pissweet!

ELEUTHERIA. Eek! (*She faints and is carried off.*)

PA UBU. Your Honour, pray don't let this trifling incident delay you in the least. Go on, please, and render us the justice which is our due.

PUBLIC PROSECUTOR. Yes, gentlemen, this monster already soiled by so many crimes . . .

COUNSEL FOR THE DEFENCE. Yes, gentlemen, this honest citizen with an irreproachable record . . .

PROSECUTOR. Having extended his vile designs by using a polishing-brush on the naked feet of his victim . . .

COUNSEL. Despite the fact that he went down on his knees to beg for mercy from this infamous trollop . . .

PROSECUTOR. Abducted her, aided and abetted by his abominable wife, Ma Ubu, forced her into a carriage . . .

COUNSEL. Found himself locked with his virtuous spouse in the boot of a carriage . . .

PA UBU (*to his* DEFENDING COUNSEL). Hey, you there, Sir, shut up please! You're telling lies and preventing this assembly from hearing all about our magnificent achievements. Yes, gentlemen, try to keep your nearoles open and stop kicking up such a row: we have been king of Poland and of Aragon, we have massacred more persons than can be counted, we have levied triple taxes, we dreamed solely of bloodletting, cash extortion, flaying alive and assassination; we performed the debraining ceremony regularly every Sunday on a convenient hillock in the suburbs, surrounded by an audience of wooden horses and coconut-shy operators. – Being very tidy in our habits, we have filed and disposed of these old criminal cases, but since then we have slain Mister Pissale, a fact to which he will certainly bear witness himself, and we have lashed Mister Pissweet here unmercifully with a whip, as you can see from the scars on our body, although this performance prevented us from hearing the sound of Miss Pissale's ringing . . . For all these reasons, we command you, gentlemen, our judge and prosecutor, to sentence us to the harshest punishment you can think up between you, so that we get what we deserve for our crimes: do not condemn us to death, however, because then you would have to vote exorbitant taxes for the construction of a sufficiently enormous guillotine. We rather fancy ourselves as a galley-slave, a fine green cap on our head, foddered at State expense and occupying our leisure hours in petty tasks. As for Ma Ubu . . .

MA UBU. But . . .

PA UBU. Hush, sweet child – . . . she will embroider designs on carpet-slippers. And as we don't want to have to worry about our future, we trust that our sentence will be for life and that our country holiday may be arranged at some warm, sunny seaside resort.

PISSWEET (to PISSALE). So there really are people who can't stand the idea of being free!

PISSALE. Listen, you, I know you want to marry my niece, but frankly I could never sacrifice her to a man dishonoured by the name 'Pissweet'.

PISSWEET. And I would never dream of marrying a girl whose uncle is unworthy even of the name 'Pissale'!

USHER. The Court is considering its verdict.

MA UBU. Pa Ubu, I'm afraid these people are going to acquit you; you did wrong not to say the Word to them in the first place.

PISSWEET (to PISSALE). Well, I'm glad to see we agree.

PISSALE. Come to my arms, nephew-in-law.

JUDGE. The Court has deliberated. Pa Ubu, do you know how to row?

PA UBU. I don't know if I know or not. But I do know how to give orders which will make a sailing-ship or a steamboat go in any direction I like, backwards, sideways or even down-wards.

JUDGE. That's beside the point. – The Court condemns Francis Ubu, known as Pa Ubu, to penal servitude for life as a galley-slave. He is sentenced to have a ball and chain fastened to each ankle while in prison and then to be sent to join the first available shipment of convicts for the galleys of Soliman, Sultan of the Turks. – The Court condemns his accomplice, known as Ma Ubu, to be fitted with one ball and chain, and to suffer solitary confinement for life in her prison.

PISSWEET ⎫
PISSALE ⎬ Hurrah for freedom!

PA UBU ⎫
MA UBU ⎬ Hurrah for slavery!

SCENE THREE

The prison. PA UBU *and* MA UBU *enter, their entrance being preceded by the sound of the iron balls they are dragging behind them.*

MA UBU. – Oh, Pa Ubu, you get prettier every day. You were just born to wear a green cap and to sport manacles!

PA UBU. What's more, madam, they are in the process right now of forging my high-ranking iron collar!

MA UBU. What does it look like, Pa Ubu?

PA UBU. Madam my female, do you remember the tall gold collar on General Laski's uniform? – you should do, you spent your whole time in Poland ogling him. – Well, this is an identical creation, except that it's not gilded, since you advised me to be economical. Oh, it's all solid stuff, you know, the same iron as our balls and chains are made of; none of that sloppy tin-can stuff – real flat-iron!

MA UBU. Stupid idiot! The iron balls you're dragging behind you are a ridiculous invention; you'll trip over them sooner or later, Pa Ubu. What a din!

PA UBU. Not ridiculous at all, Ma Ubu. With the aid of these

adornments I'll be able to tread on your toes all the more
effectively!

MA UBU. Ow, no, let me off, please, Mister Ubu, Sir.

SCENE FOUR

A salon in an academy set aside for pious exhibitions, in which
several OLD MAIDS *are scurrying around.*

FIRST OLD MAID. Yes, indeed, ladies, a big fat gentleman has
arrived in this Free Country of ours, swearing that he intends
to wait on everyone, be everyone's servant, and use his arts
to turn all the Free Men into Masters. And when anyone
has objected to this he's simply stuffed them into his pocket
or into the boot of any passing carriage.

SECOND OLD MAID. Yes, and that's not all. On my way back
from church just now, I got caught in a huge crowd outside
the prison – you know, that crumbling old edifice that is only
being preserved as an ancient monument, and has a member
of the Académie Française as gaoler. Pa Ubu is being kept
there at the State's expense, until enough other people have
also merited the honours of judicial procedure and make up
a presentable convoy for the galleys of Soliman. That won't
take long: they've already had to raze several districts to the
ground, simply to build extensions to the prisons.

ALL. May the heavens protect this house of ours!

SCENE FIVE

The same. BROTHER BUNG.

BROTHER BUNG. Peace be with you!

FIRST OLD MAID. Oh, goodness gracious, I didn't hear you
knock!

BUNG. It is not fitting that messengers of sweetness and light
should cause the least disturbance anywhere, even by
knocking ever so gently. I come to beseech your customary

charity on behalf of a new set of poor people: the poor prisoners.

SECOND OLD MAID. The poor prisoners?!

FIRST OLD MAID. But the poor are all Free Men, wandering around and hammering with their crutches on every door in the street, kicking up such a rumpus that everyone rushes to the window and leans out to watch what's going on, so that giving them alms practically becomes a public ceremony.

BUNG (*holding out his hand*). For the poor prisoners! Pa Ubu has threatened to barricade himself inside his prison, together with Ma Ubu and his large band of followers, unless the authorities provide him with the twelve meals a day he needs for his sustenance. He has declared his intention of throwing everybody out on to the street, stark naked, in the middle of winter – which he predicts will be a very hard one – while he'll remain well sheltered inside, surrounded by his henchmen, with nothing more to do than cut his claws with a little saw and watch Ma Ubu embroider carpet-slippers to keep the convicts' iron balls warm!

ALL. Twelve meals! Cutting his claws! Slippers for iron balls! We won't give him a sou, certainly not!

BUNG. In that case, peace be with you, sisters! Others will soon knock louder, and you will certainly hear *them*!

He goes off. Enter POLICEMEN *and* WRECKERS. *The* PIOUS OLD MAIDS *flee. The* WRECKERS *smash all the window panes and fix iron bars into the frames, cart off the furniture, replace it with straw, then moisten the straw with water from a watering-can. The salon is entirely transformed into the prison décor of the following scene:*

SCENE SIX

The prison. PA UBU, *in chains*; PISSWEET.

PA UBU. Hey there, Pissweet, my friend! Just look at you: no roof over your head, roaming the streets with your three ragamuffins. I suppose you've come to beg for assistance

from our phynance vehicle? Well, we shan't even lend you
the diligence you'll need to consummate your wedding night
with Miss Pissale. She is free too, her uncle is *her* only
prison – very leaky when raining! Look at me, now! I never
go out. I wear a beautiful ball on each foot, and to save them
from rusting in this damp atmosphere I've spared no expense
and had them liberally coated with glue, so now they refuse
to budge an inch!

PISSWEET. Ahrgg! I've had enough of you, Pa Ubu, I'm
going to grab you by the scruff of your neck and drag you
out of this shell of yours.

PA UBU. I'm afraid, my good man, that your single idea of
freedom will never make a good snail-fork, which is a two-
pronged instrument. In any case, I'm fastened to the wall.
Good night. Since our astrological calculations have indicated to us that you'll be sleeping under the stars tonight,
we have ordered the street-lamps to be lit: they will supple-
ment the starlight sufficiently for you to be able to get a
really clear view of cold, hunger and emptiness. Ah well, it's
our bedtime, I see. The gaoler will show you out.

SCENE SEVEN

The same. THE GAOLER.

GAOLER. Closing time!

SCENE EIGHT

The passageway of a seraglio. SOLIMAN, *his* VIZIER, *followed
by attendants.*

VIZIER. Sire, the Free Country has at last confirmed to Your
Majesty the despatch of the tribute which it has taken them
so long to amass. The authorities say the convoy comprises
two hundred convicts, including the illustrious Pa Ubu, who
is fatter than the fattest of Your eunuchs, although as far as
his virility is concerned he claims to be married to the no less
notorious Ma Ubu.

SOLIMAN. Yes, I have heard of this man known as Pa Ubu. I'm told he was once king of Poland and Aragon, and had some amazing adventures. But he eats pig-meat and pisses standing up. He must be either a madman or a heretic!

VIZIER. Sire, he is deeply versed in many branches of occult knowledge and might prove useful as a source of amusement for Your Majesty. He's an expert in astrology and the art of navigation.

SOLIMAN. Good. He'll row all the better in my galleys.

Act Four

SCENE ONE

FIRST FREE MAN (*to the* SECOND). Where are you off to, comrade? To drill, same as every morning? Hey, I suspect you're obeying.

SECOND FREE MAN. The Corporal has ordered me never to turn up for drill at this particular hour. But I'm a Free Man, so I go every morning.

FIRST *and* THIRD FREE MEN (*together*). So that's why we keep meeting by accident every morning – so that we can all disobey together as regular as clockwork.

SECOND FREE MAN. But the Corporal didn't show up today.

THIRD FREE MAN. He's free not to come.

FIRST FREE MAN. And since it's raining . . .

SECOND FREE MAN. We are free not to enjoy being rained on.

FIRST FREE MAN. You see what I told you: you're both becoming obedient.

SECOND FREE MAN. It's more like it's the Corporal what's becoming obedient. He often misses our indiscipline drills these days.

THIRD FREE MAN. Whereas we're standing guard in front of this prison just for the fun of it, in these here sentry-boxes.

SECOND FREE MAN. And they're free too!

THIRD FREE MAN. Besides, we've been strictly forbidden to take shelter inside the sentry-boxes.

FIRST FREE MAN. You are the Free Men!

SECOND *and* THIRD FREE MEN (*together*). Yea, yea, we are the Free Men!

SCENE TWO

The same. LORD CORNHOLER, *his valet* JACK.

LORD CORNHOLER. Oh, really, the only noteworthy thing about this town is that it's built entirely of houses, like any other town, and that all its houses look exactly like houses anywhere else. Too, too boring really. Oh, but I say, surely this must be the King's palace ahead of us. – Jack!

The valet bows.

Do look up the word 'palace' in the dictionary, dear boy.

JACK (*reading out*). Palace: edifice constructed of blocks of granite, decorated with iron bars. Royal Palace, the Louvre: similar model, but with a gate in front presided over by guards whose function it is to ensure that no one gets in.

CORNHOLER. Well, it looks all right, but just to make sure, Jack, ask this guard if it really is the King's palace.

JACK (*to the* FIRST FREE MAN). Soldier, is this the King's palace?

SECOND FREE MAN (*to the* FIRST). Truth compels you to admit that we haven't got a king and so this building can't be the King's palace. We are the Free Men!

FIRST FREE MAN (*to the* SECOND). Truth compels me . . . ? Not at all. Being Free Men, we shouldn't take orders even from truth itself. – Yes, mister foreigner, sir, this building is in fact the King's palace.

CORNHOLER. Oh goody goody! Here's a big tip for you. – Jack!

The valet bows.

Go and knock on the door and ask if I may have audience of the King.

The valet knocks.

SCENE THREE

The same. THE GAOLER.

GAOLER. Sorry, gentlemen, no entry.

CORNHOLER. Oh! this gentleman must be the gentleman who guards the King. Well, he shan't get a tip from me since he won't let English tourists in. (*To the* FIRST FREE MAN). Do you think you could persuade His Majesty to come to the door? I should adore to see the King in the flesh, and if he'll do me this favour I'll give him a big tip as a reward.

THIRD FREE MAN (*to the* FIRST). In the first place, there's no king and no queen, either inside there or anywhere else in this country for that matter; in the second place, the people who are inside aren't allowed out.

FIRST FREE MAN. You're right. (*To* LORD CORNHOLER.) Mister foreigner, sir, the king and queen who are in there emerge with their retinue every day to accept tips from English tourists!

CORNHOLER. Oh, hurray! I am grateful to you for the information. Here's another tip for you to drink my health. — Jack! Pitch our tent and open some tins of corned beef. We shall camp here while awaiting audience of the King and the opportunity to kiss the hand of Her Gracious Majesty the Queen!

SCENE FOUR

The prison yard. PA UBU, MA UBU, CONVICTS, GUARDS.

THE CONVICTS. Hurrah for slavery! Hurrah for Pa Ubu!

PA UBU. Ma Ubu, do you happen to have a piece of string I could use to tie the links of my chains together more securely? The balls are so heavy I'm afraid the chains may break when I try to walk.

MA UBU. Stupid clot!

PA UBU. Look, my iron collar's coming undone and the man-acles are so big they're slipping off my wrists. If I'm not careful I'll end up at liberty, stripped of these fine trappings, deprived of my escort and other honours, and forced to pay my own expenses!

GUARD. Hey, Mister Ubu, Sir, there's your green cap flying over the windmills.

PA UBU. What windmills? My headquarters is no longer that windmill on the hill in the Ukraine from which I commanded my army. Oh no, I don't intend to get shot at ever again. But I miss my dear old phynance charger.

MA UBU. You were always complaining he wasn't strong enough to carry you.

PA UBU. Horn of Ubu! That was because he never got anything to eat! It's true that my iron balls don't eat either, and wouldn't complain if you stole from *them*. Besides, I no longer have the account books in which I used to study your embezzlements. But enough of these considerations! From now on it will be those in charge of the Turkish galleys who will be robbing me, Ma Ubu, not you any longer. Farewell, Ma Ubu! We really should have a band to play stirring military music at our parting.

MA UBU. Look, here comes the escort of guards in their beautiful yellow-braided uniforms.

PA UBU. Ah well, from now on we shall have to content ourselves with the monotonous clanking of our chains. Farewell once more, Ma Ubu. Soon I shall be regaled by the sound of splashing waves and creaking oars! My Gaoler will look after you.

MA UBU. Farewell, Pa Ubu. If you should decide to come back any time for a little peace and quiet, you'll find me in the same stoutly-built little room, and by then I'll have embroidered you a beautiful pair of slippers. Ah, these farewells are too heart-breaking! I'll accompany you at least as far as the door!

PA UBU, MA UBU *and the* CONVICTS *move off towards the door at the back of the stage, dragging their chains behind them and jostling and tripping over each other.*

SCENE FIVE

The square in front of the prison. LORD CORNHOLER, *his valet* JACK, THE THREE FREE MEN, THE GAOLER. THE GAOLER *removes the bars, draws the bolts and unlocks all the locks on the outside of the door.*

CORNHOLER. Jack! Strike the tent and sweep up all these empty tins of corned beef, so that we can receive Their Majesties with due ceremony!

FIRST FREE MAN (*dead drunk, waving an empty bottle*). Long live the King! Long live the King! Hurrah for the King!

SECOND FREE MAN. Idiot! That's Pa Ubu and Ma Ubu!

THIRD FREE MAN. Psst! Shut up, and we'll get our share of tips and free drinks!

SECOND FREE MAN. Me shut up? We're Free Men, aren't we! (*At the top of his voice.*) Long live the King! Hey! Hurrah for the King!

The door opens. The GUARDS *start coming out.*

SCENE SIX

The same. GUARDS, PA UBU, MA UBU.

PA UBU (*stopping in amazement in the doorway, at the head of the flight of steps leading down to the square, with* MA UBU *at his side*). Hornstrumpot, I must be losing my mind! What's the meaning of all this shouting and banging about? And all these drunken louts, they're as bad as the ones back in Poland! Help! They're going to crown me king again and beat me black and blue!

MA UBU. These fine upstanding individuals are not drunk at all. On the contrary. See, here's one all decked out in lace trimmings and gold braid who's just come up to beg the honour of kissing my regal hand!

CORNHOLER. Jack! Come back here, you naughty boy! First look up in the dictionary the words 'King' and 'Queen'.

JACK (*reading out*). King, Queen: he or she who wears a ceremonial metal collar around the neck, and ornaments such as chains and cords at the wrists and ankles. Carries an orb representing the world . . .

CORNHOLER. The king of this country is a great, fat, double king! He has *two* orbs, and drags them with his feet instead of carrying them.

JACK (*reading out*). King of France, similar model. Wears a cloak bearing a design of fleur-de-lys buckled at the shoulder.

CORNHOLER. This king's shoulder is quite bare, and there's a beautiful red fleur-de-lys inlaid into the skin itself. He must be a real, hereditary king of ancient lineage! Long live the King!

JACK *and* THREE FREE MEN (*together*). Long live the King! Hurrah for the King!

PA UBU. God Almighty! I'm lost! Hornstrumpot, where can I hide?

MA UBU. You've made a fine mess of your plans for being a slave! You wanted to polish these people's feet, and now these same people are kissing your hands! And they don't seem any more squeamish about it than you do!

PA UBU. Madam our wife, watch out for your nearoles! We'll inflict severe punishment when we have more leisure. Right now, we're going to send this mob graciously on its way, just like in the good old days when our royal person's bumboozle overflowed the edges of the throne of Wenceslas . . . – Hornboodle, pack of guttersnipes! Bugger off this instant, all of you! We don't like people creating an uproar in our presence, no one has ever dared to do so before, and we don't intend to let you be the ones to start! So shut up and piss off!

Everyone withdraws most respectfully, with repeated cries of 'Long live the King'.

SCENE SEVEN

PA UBU, MA UBU, THE CONVICTS, *among the latter the* LEADER OF THE CONVICTS *and* BROTHER BUNG. THE CONVICTS *have sneaked up behind* PA UBU *during his peroration, and are now sprawling all over the stage.*

MA UBU. Ah, they've gone at last. But what's this bunch of riffraff doing here?

PA UBU. These are friends, Ma Ubu, our prison colleagues, all disciples and loyal henchmen.

CONVICTS. Long live the King!

PA UBU. What, again! Quiet, I say, or by my green candle I'll beat you all up good and proper!

LEADER OF THE CONVICTS. Don't be angry with us, Pa Ubu. We are addressing you by your title because it is eternally linked with your name, and thus we are demonstrating our faithful attachment to your glorious past. Besides, we hope that between friends and colleagues, so to speak, your innate modesty may yet permit us to boast of your exploits!

MA UBU. Oh, what a beautiful speech!

PA UBU. My friends, I am deeply touched. However, I'm doling out no money . . .

MA UBU. Ah, I should hope not!

PA UBU. Silence, clownish female! . . . because we aren't in Poland any longer. But I wish to make due recognition of your loyalty and efficiency by handing out a few promotions – that is, if you won't refuse to accept such honours from our hand – our royal hand, since it pleases you to insist on our title. The chief advantage of this distribution of honours is that it will reduce the queue of those fighting to acquire precedence in carrying segments of the great chain of office which stretches out behind our bumboozle! You there, venerable Leader of our noble Convicts, you old embezzler, you, we hereby create you Grand Treasurer of our Phynances! You over there, the legless cripple imprisoned for forgery and murder, we appoint you Commander-in-Chief!

And you, Brother Bung, who share a small section of our
great iron rosary, too, for lechery, extortion, and wilful
destruction of private property, shall be our Grand Almoner!
You, convicted poisoner, from now on you're our personal
physician! And all the rest of you, thieves, bandits, brain-
extruders, I name you all without exception gallant Craptains
of our Pschittanarmy!

Act Five

SCENE ONE

The square in front of the prison. ELEUTHERIA, PISSALE, PISSWEET, THE FREE MEN, PEOPLE.

PISSWEET. Forward, comrades! Hurrah for freedom! That fat slab of galley-fodder, Pa Ubu, has been taken away with the rest of the chain-gang, the prisons are empty, and nobody's left but Ma Ubu who's unsewing mailbags and converting them into carpet-slippers. We are free to do what we want, even to obey. We are free to go anywhere we choose, even to prison! Slavery is the only true freedom!

ALL. Hurrah for Pissweet!

PISSWEET. In response to your pleas, I agree to take over command. Forward! Let's break into the prisons and abolish freedom!

ALL. Hurrah, hurrah! Let's all obey. Forward! Off to the prison!

SCENE TWO

The same. MA UBU, THE GAOLER.

PISSWEET. Ha! there's Ma Ubu, using the bars of her cell as a mask. She looked better without the disguise . . . ah, what a pretty little girl she was once upon a time.

MA UBU. Vile Pissweet!

GAOLER. No entry here, gentlemen. Who are you, anyway?

Shouts, yells and jostling.

Free Men, are you? On your way, then, go on, move along there!

FIRST FREE MAN. Let's smash the bars of the cells!

SECOND FREE MAN. No, no, if we did that we'd no longer feel at home once we got in!

THIRD FREE MAN. Let's break the door down!

ELEUTHERIA. Yes, please do. I've been tugging at the bell-rope for hours, but my concierge still hasn't opened up.

MA UBU (*furiously*). Go on, knock, I'll open up all right!

She reaches through the bars of her cell window, clutching a stone jug, and bangs PISSALE *on the head with it, splitting him neatly in half from top to toe.*

PISSALE (*both halves in unison*). Don't be alarmed, dear child. You now have two uncles.

ALL. Aha! Home at last. In we go.

The door gives way, and they all pour in. THE GAOLER *flees.* MA UBU *emerges. The door slams shut on her ball and chain, trapping her. But* ELEUTHERIA *slips her arm through the prison's wicket-gate, and cuts the chain with a pair of nail-scissors.*

SCENE THREE

The convoy making its way across Slaveonia. GUARDS, CON-VICTS, PA UBU.

PA UBU. Hornstrumpot, we're perishing! Mister Boss, Sir, be good enough to continue dragging us along by our chain so as to take some of the weight off our ball. And you, Mister Guard, Sir, pray put our manacles back on, so that we won't have to go to the trouble of clasping our hands behind our back as is our usual custom when going out for a stroll. And please screw our iron collar tighter round our neck so that we won't catch cold!

GUARD. Cheer up, Pa Ubu, we've nearly reached the port where the galleys are waiting.

PA UBU. We deplore more than ever the fact that the state of our finances still does not permit us to acquire our own private Black Maria. As it is, our iron balls absolutely refuse to walk ahead of us and pull us after them, so we have had to make the entire journey pulling them ourselves by means of our feet, and even then they have insisted on stopping at frequent intervals, presumably to relieve themselves.

SCENE FOUR

The same. THE GAOLER.

GAOLER (*running up*). All is lost, Pa Ubu!

PA UBU. What, again! Look, I'm not a king any more, you nincompoop!

GAOLER. The Masters have revolted! The Free Men have become slaves, I've been thrown out, and Ma Ubu has been abducted from her prison cell. To prove the truth of what I'm saying: look, here's Ma Ubu's iron ball . . .

The ball is trundled in in a wheelbarrow.

. . . which she's been judged unworthy to wear, and which, in any case, broke its chain by itself, refusing to follow her any longer!

PA UBU (*stuffs the ball into his pocket*). Oof! to hell with these watches without watch-chains! Any heavier and it would have bust my pocket!

GAOLER. The Masters have moved their wives and children into the prisons. They've invaded the arsenals and are having a hard time finding enough cannon-balls to rivet to their legs as a badge of slavery. What's more, they're planning to get into Soliman's galleys ahead of you and occupy your seats.

ALL THE GUARDS. I'm joining the rebellion! – Hurrah for slavery! – Yah, we've had enough of this! We want to be slaves too, bugger it!

PA UBU (*to a* GUARD). Here, we present you with our own ball, pray don't bother to thank us. We shall ask you to return it to us after we have had a little rest.

He gives the balls to carry to the GUARDS *on either side of him.* THE CONVICTS, *giving in to the entreaties of the* GUARDS, *load them with their chains. A confused din can be heard in the distance.*

GUARDS *and* CONVICTS. Oh! oh! it's the rebel Masters!

PA UBU. Come now, gentlemen! Let's pluck up our courage by both handles. I see that you are armed and ready to face the enemy valiantly. As for ourself, now that we are once more light-footed, we intend to go quietly on our way without awaiting the arrival of these people who are, we fear, evilly disposed towards us. Luckily for us, it seems from that loud clanking noise I hear that they are heavily loaded with chains.

GAOLER. No, that's the noise of cannon! They've got artillery, Pa Ubu.

PA UBU. Oh! I'm scared to death. Let's get back to the comfort of prison and carpet-slippers!

Cannons are wheeled on and surround the stage.

SCENE FIVE

The same. PISSWEET, THE FREE MEN *in chains.*

PISSWEET. Surrender, Pa Ubu! Hand over your iron collar, manacles and chains! Be free! We're going to strip you stark naked and show the world what you look like without your jewellery!

PA UBU. Oh yes, Mister Pissweet? Just you try and catch me ... (*He runs off.*)

PISSWEET. Load the cannons. Fire on that big barrel of cowardice!

THIRD FREE MAN. Let's obey. All together now, on the count of three!

FIRST FREE MAN. Hey, Corporal, the cannon-ball didn't go off.

SECOND FREE MAN. Too true. It's the third Free Man's leg that went off!

FIRST FREE MAN. Left foot forward, as usual, the clumsy oaf.

SECOND FREE MAN. There are no cannon-balls left in the battery, Corporal. We used them all up attaching them to our ankles as symbols of our newly-won slavery.

PA UBU (*reappears*). Don't worry! Here's Ma Ubu's ball, it's been weighing down our pocket and we're glad to get rid of it. (*He hurls it at* PISSWEET *and scores a direct hit.*) Now try some of this grape-shot! (*He massacres the* FREE MEN *by swinging a line of chained* GUARDS *at them.*)

FREE MEN. Help! Run for your lives!

They run away, dragging their chains behind them and pursued by the now unencumbered CONVICTS. *From time to time,* PA UBU *grabs hold of the end of the chain, jerking the whole file to a halt.*

GAOLER. We're saved, we're saved! Look, there are the Turkish galleys!

The rout is halted. SOLIMAN, *his* VIZIER *and his retinue appear at the back of the stage.*

SCENE SIX

The headquarters of the Turks. SOLIMAN, *the* VIZIER.

SOLIMAN. Vizier, have you taken delivery of two hundred slaves?

VIZIER. Sire, I have signed a receipt for that many slaves, since this was the number stipulated in our agreement with the Free Country, but the convoy in fact consists of more than two thousand heads. I just don't understand. Most of them are ridiculously festooned with chains and are loudly demanding fetters and leg-irons, which I understand even less, unless this is their way of showing their eagerness to participate in the honour of rowing in Your Majesty's galleys.

SOLIMAN. How about Pa Ubu?

VIZIER. Pa Ubu claims his balls and chains were stolen from him on the way. He's in a terrible rage and threatens to stuff everyone in his pocket. At the moment he's breaking all the oars and smashing the benches while testing their solidity.

SOLIMAN. Enough! Treat him with the greatest respect. It's not that I'm afraid of his violent nature ... Now that I've seen him in person, I realize how far greater he is even than report had it. I was so impressed by his noble air and majestic presence, in fact, that I made some private enquiries which have yielded an additional title to fame for him. – Know then the real identity of this Pa Ubu who has been sent to me as a slave: he is my own long-lost brother, abducted many years ago by French pirates, and kept at hard labour in various convict prisons, whereby he was able to work his way up to the eminent position of King of Aragon and later King of Poland! Kiss the ground beneath his hands, but do not on any account reveal to him this astonishing news, for if he got an inkling of it he'd immediately install himself here in my empire with his whole family, and he'd be bound to gobble up my fortune in no time at all. Shove him on board a ship, and be quick about it. It doesn't matter where the ship's bound for, so long as we get him out of this country. See to it.

VIZIER. Sire, I obey.

SCENE SEVEN

PA UBU, MA UBU.

MA UBU. Pa Ubu, these people are herding us on board like cattle.

PA UBU. So much the better. I'll be able to supervise the bull-pschitt while all the others row.

MA UBU. You've not had much of a success as a slave, have you, Pa Ubu? Nobody wants to be your master any longer.

PA UBU. What d'you mean? Things couldn't be better. Private sources have revealed to me that my Strumpot is huger than the whole world, and therefore worthier of my services. From now on I shall be the slave of my Strumpot.

MA UBU. Ah, you're so right, as usual, Pa Ubu.

SCENE EIGHT

The leading galley. PA UBU, MA UBU, THE GAOLER, ALL THE CHARACTERS *who have appeared during the play, chained to the benches as* GALLEY-SLAVES.

PA UBU. Look at all that greenery, Ma Ubu! You'd think we were in a cow-pasture.

CONVICTS (*chanting in rhythm as they row*). *Let's mow the great meadow with sweeps of our scythes!*

PA UBU. Yes, green is the colour of hope. Let us await a happy ending to all our adventures.

MA UBU. What strange music! They're all singing through their noses: they must have caught cold from the early-morning dew!

GAOLER. Just to please you, sir and madam, I've replaced the galley-slaves' usual muzzles with kazoos.

CONVICTS (*chanting in rhythm*). *Let's mow the great meadow with sweeps of our scythes!*

GAOLER. Would you care to take command of the ship, Pa Ubu?

PA UBU. Oh no! Even though you've chucked me out of this country and are taking me God knows where as a passenger in this galley, I still remain Ubu Enchained, Ubu slave, and I'm not giving any orders ever again. That way people will obey me all the more promptly.

MA UBU. We're getting farther and farther away from France, Pa Ubu.

PA UBU. Ah, my sweet child, don't you worry your pretty head about our destination. It will certainly be a country extra-ordinary enough to be worthy of our presence, since we are being transported there in a trireme equipped with an extra bank of oars – not just three, but four!